Wisdom and Practices

of the Ancient Faith

by

Father Alphonse and Rachel Goettmann

Translated by Theodore J. Nottingham

ISBN 9780985907433

Translated from the original French,

Sagesse et Pratiques du Christianisme

Biblical quotations from the New King James Version

TABLE OF CONTENTS

Foreword   3

Translator's Preface   15

Introduction   17

I. The Call of Silence   21

II. The Book of Our Destiny   35

III. The Surprising Practice of Praise   59

IV. The Icon: Transparence to Beauty   79

V. At the Source of Life   125

VI. Paths of Healing   169

VII. Toward a Transparent Consciousness   231

FOREWORD

by Dr. Charles Ashanin

What is Christianity? This is a perennial question about which there are many divergent views among Christians themselves, which also explains the variety of ecclesial bodies within the Christian fold. Broadly speaking, they fall in three major groups: Orthodox, Roman Catholic and Protestant. Although these three divisions came into being during the second millenium of Christian history, their origins can be traced to the very beginnings of Christianity and to the New Testament itself. For instance, the Synoptic Gospels (Matthew, Mark and Luke) are understood to interpret the major event of the Christian Faith, Jesus the Christ, within the context of history. The claim is made that these Gospels teach that He provides history with the true knowledge of how human beings should live in order to find fulfillment as social beings.

In this view, Jesus is an enlightened teacher and a better philosopher in comparison to other great luminaries in history. He provides humankind with better information about God and human nature. The key word here is information, for by following His teaching, humankind would finally realize the real *homonoia*, universal concord and social harmony. This is what humanity has been seeking through what the Greeks called *Padeia*, the education of humanity as beings endowed with reason. But this effort seemed to many to be an illusive dream and by the time of the rise of Christianity, philosophy which was thought to bring about *homonoia*, the universal accord, was not capable of being able to realize this ideal. However, in the minds of many people who dreamed of *homonoia*, the appearance of Christianity seemed to be capable of achieving what ancient philosophy had failed to do and they pursued its realization by espousing the new religion. This "philosophical" view of the Faith became dominant in the Western Latin tradition of Christianity (i.e., Roman Catholic and Protestant). The aim of this new Christian Society was to change history by realizing the dream of ancient *homonoia*. This was to be achieved through bringing humanity in conformity to the will of God so that His reign might supplant that of Caesar.

But this was not the only tradition of the Christian Faith. Along with the Synoptic tradition of Christianity and the interpretation of Christianity as our Divine *information*, there also stands the tradition of the Gospel of Saint John, as well as the writings of Saint Paul, which explicitly state that the Messiah Jesus is not just a bearer of Divine information, but of *Divine Revelation*. Jesus, the Christ, does not only inform us about God. He reveals God. This is not a matter of quibbling with words. Divine information and Divine Revelation are not the same. The latter does not so much aim at changing history but seeks to transform human beings. In other words, human beings are not educated to create a better social order, but are instead incorporated into the Divine life.

According to the Johannine and Pauline traditions, Jesus the Messiah came into history and not out of history. He came from the bosom of the Father in order to help human beings return to their Father from whom they have alienated themselves. In this vision of Christianity, God acts directly upon each human person, and not through intermediaries. According to Christianity as Divine information, intermediaries are necessary to the process of educating humankind for the Christian social order. According to John and Paul, God is directly raising sons and daughters to inherit the Kingdom prepared **"before the foundation of the world"** (Jn 17:24).

There is no question here of a new enlightened society as a center of Divine concern but rather an issue of the *hagios*, the saint. The saint is born "not of blood nor of the will of the flesh, but of God" (Jn 1:13). God reveals Himself to the saints directly through the Holy Spirit who is God's own unveiling of Himself to His children as their Creator and Savior. As a consequence of God's disclosure, there comes into being the communion of the Redeemed, i.e., the saints who are the Church, not as an organization but as the Divine-human organ, the mystical Body of Christ. Therefore, the Church is not so much an "observed" reality but is a spiritually discerned reality. This is important to remember because the Church thus understood is not dependent on the ambiguities and predicaments of the world but on the mercy of God, This is also the meaning of the words of Jesus: **"Be of good cheer, I have overcome the world"** (Jn 16:33). In other words, the Church is the Divine Creation in which God indwells in His saints.

The saints are God's own "household" with whom, in the words of the Medieval Byzantine writer Nicolas Cabasilas (14th century), "God shares His Kingdom, not as His servants but as His own family" (*Life in Christ*). In this vision of Christianity, the Church is essentially a communion rather than a community of like-minded people, for it is this communion (i.e., the bond of love between God in Christ and His saints) that makes the Church as a visible social organ possible. In this view of the Church, primacy belongs to the saints as God's anointed friends and not to the *cleros*, who are only servants of God's people. This point is clearly underlined by the authors in the sixth chapter of this book. Structures and "principalities" in the Church exist for the sake of the saints and not the other way around as the proponents of the militant Church affirm. God's Kingdom, though not as yet universally acknowledged, is universally revealed. There is a beautiful passage in the last chapter of this book which bears witness to this: "Through Christ, God has entered into history, that is, into time and space. Henceforth, there is not a single place or moment which is not filled with His

Presence."

The two interpretations of Christianity continue to coexist in the Church. The Church of Christ the Teacher may be called the Church militant. It believes itself in duty bound to bring Christ's Kingdom upon earth. Its monuments are great ecclesiastical establishments, such as bureaucracies, educational enterprises, missionary and social agencies. Its leaders are Christ's vicars and deputies, as if Christ were absent from His Church. Here the Church is the visible presence meant to counteract the power of this world with its own power. A good Christian in this understanding of the Church, therefore, is one who loyally supports the ecclesiastical system. The militant Church competes with the powers of the world for influence in the world. Its philosophers are theologians and canon lawyers, the guardians of its discipline. Its founding father is Saint Cyprian (died 258) who argued that the unity of the Church is based on the Episcopate holding the common profession of Faith. As a former Roman magistrate, he simply transposed the Roman law which undergirded the Empire into the idea of Christian Faith where bishops did the same for the Church.

With Cyprian, the clergy became the new magistrates of the Church as the New Society. The Gospel simply became the New Law which was renamed the Divine Law. The fathers of the Church are its great legislators, Leo the First (fifth century), Gregory the Great (died 604) and Innocent III (died 1216), all were bishops of Rome. The objective, visible elements of this Church's life are the true marks of its Christianity. The subjective and inner elements are to be avoided or condemned as being suspect of heresy!

Alongside this Church of law and order there stands the Church of the Divine Revelation. Its center is not institutional but sacramental. Its patron Saint is Saint Ignatius of Antioch (martyred in 115). According to this vision of Christianity, the Kingdom of God and the union with God is its true aspiration, but this Kingdom does not come by "observation" (Lk 20:18). It is not an outward show but an inner invitation known through experience which is the intimation of the presence of the Holy Spirit in the lives of the believers.The agenda of the followers of this path is a journey through *askesis* (total surrender) in order to enter more fully into the life of Christ according to Saint Paul's saying: "It is no longer I who live, but Christ lives in me" (Ga 2:20). The pathfinders of the Way are the patriarchs, prophets, apostles, martyrs, confessors, and ascetics. This vision of Christianity centers on the person of Christ as the Axis around which their whole life revolves. They profess the Faith as taught by the Orthodox Catholic Church through the ages, but they understand that Faith not as information or doctrine to be learned, but as a way of life to be lived. They believe Christianity to be the Revelation of God, i.e. the unveiling of the divine which unites the believer in Christ with God so that the believers may live in God and God in them. This revelation must be appropriated in order to become an inner illumination.

Among Western Christians, this path has been followed by the great saints and mystics, but its true home has been chiefly the Orthodox Church for which this understanding of Christianity has been normative. This is witnessed to by the fact that to the Orthodox the only fully recognized theologians have been Saint John, the Fourth Evangelist, Gregory Nanziansus, one of the great Fathers of the Church (d. 390) and Saint Symeon the New Theologian, the great Medieval mystic (d. 1022). All three have made such an indelible impact on Orthodox

Christianity that their vision is its authentic form, so much so that if ever the Orthodox Church should depart from it, it would lose its soul and become the salt that has lost its flavor, as Jesus said, and therefore become worthless for human use.

It is not surprising that Western Christians are discovering this Orthodox Christianity of the Holy Spirit and becoming her children. Among these are the authors of this book, Father Alphonse Goettmann of the Orthodox Church of France and his wife Rachel. Inspired by gratitude to God for vouchsafing to them the understanding of this inner vision of Christianity, they present in the following pages an eloquent interpretation of this way of transformation which I venture to say will be an eye opener to every reader who is seeking to enter into communion with God through Christ, the Revealer. The authors make available in this book their own discovery of Christianity as the tradition which bears witness to the New Covenant which God has written on the hearts of believers. Human beings will no longer need to teach each other about God, for He will reveal Himself in their hearts (Jeremiah 31).

The translator, Theodore J. Nottingham, has given to the French text such English idiom that one meets the authors as honored members of both the English-speaking community and of the Christian spiritual community from whose experience they write so eloquently. *Sola Dei Gratia!*

Charles B. Ashanin, PH.D. (Glasgow)
Professor of Early Church History, Emeritus
Christian Theological Seminary

TRANSLATOR'S PREFACE

In the following pages, readers will find themselves in the light of the Christian spiritual experience that exploded into the world two millennia ago. Early Christianity called for a vivid personal transformation among its adherents. A new way of being was found, one characterized by a self-transcending and all consuming love. Spiritual reality was unveiled as union with the Christ—the *Anointed One* who himself was at one with the unfathomable I AM of creation. This union regenerated individual personalities thoroughly and completely.

The wisdom of the early teachers, preserved in the spiritual traditions of Eastern Orthodox Christianity, were amazingly insightful and pragmatic. These early Church Fathers were informed by the light of vaster awareness and vaster love. They called it the indwelling of the uncreated. The authors of this book, Alphonse and Rachel

15

Goettmann, are living examples of the power of illumination available through these ancient traditions.

Here is found an utterly self-transcending love, that merger with the divine goodness which compels human beings to loving participation in the world. Here is encountered the warmth of souls on fire and their awareness of the presence of the living God in every moment.

The reader is presented with the tools for this radical transformation. Surely, no one should be surprised by the seemingly rigorous asceticism required for such an ultimate, all-inclusive task. But we are all invited to discover the joy that is liberated through a certain discipline of living. It is not so much a matter of harsh physical control as it is a rechanneling of one's attention and commitments in daily life.

All seekers of spiritual awakening will find in this book instructions to guide them into their own inner furnace. There the new person is forged, made aware of his or her true nature, and alive in God's love.

Theodore J. Nottingham

INTRODUCTION

Through a secret yearning, we human beings are today sensing that we are made for a joy and fullness of life completely different from the artificial paradise offered in myriad ways by our society. Tired of theories, promises which never come through, and religious teachings based merely on morality and good conduct, we have turned toward the distant East. But this has only led us into traditions which are not our own. Returning from this search, or having never undertaken it, we are now bombarded by endless propositions which all pretend to have the answer to our fundamental questions: how to live happily, and deeper still, how not to die.

There are more and more persons now turning to Christianity, often after having rejected it. But then they find themselves faced with another question: can we overstep centuries of historical deviation and truly rediscover the Christ and the tradition of the apostles? The answer to this fundamental question is already lived by many of our contemporaries. Christianity reveals itself to them in the power it held for the first Christians, not as a system or a religion with its structures and bureaucracies, but as a concrete Path of transformation. The **"Come and follow Me"** of Christ resonates today as it did yesterday and they become disciples of the Master whom they follow intoxicated with joy. This joy was not promised for "another world" only, or in some "afterlife," but here and now! Christ resurrected means that He is alive *now,* and no joy can be greater than an encounter with Him. Faith is not a cold intellectual adherence to truths which must be believed, but an experience of *fire* which divinizes us when we come in contact with this burning Presence.

"Come and see" (John 1:39) says the Christ to all who seek, for **"I am the Way"** (John 14:6). The Way is therefore both Himself and the path of reaching the goal. It is actual physical experience, or it does not take place. God, who takes the path of the body to experience humanity, shows us clearly that it is through the body that we must experience God. This is the very logic of incarnation!

In this book, we will consider the fundamental practices of the Christian experience. They are backed by two thousand years of history and a sea of witnesses who, down through the ages, have journeyed on this path that has led them to the summits of wisdom and holiness. The difficulty in the presentation of these "methods" is their inevitable and artificial juxtaposition when they only find their internal and organic coherence in the living Tradition. They are all held together as in a living organism; each element comes at a particular stage in a life that gravitates around its axis: the Christ.

That is why we will use a method which will make it possible for the reader not to remain on the exterior as a spectator: the repetition of key ideas. This is a teaching in the form of a spiral, an "eating of the word" where, as in liturgical chants and the experiential method of Scripture, we become that which we "eat" continually, we "are" what we have just read rather than merely "knowing" it. Each chapter is a new approach to the unique Reality. Rather that addressing the intellect, it speaks to the heart.

If a particular passage strikes us, we must then have the courage to stop the reading. The Ancient Ones said:

when a text suddenly "speaks," it is the Spirit Himself who speaks to us, beyond concepts, through an experience which can become vivifying. The important thing is to stop reading, or we risk missing this visit from Being. Our joy is to listen. In this contemplative attitude is manifested the work of life within us, revealing its very mystery to the one who listens deeply. The person who lets himself be touched in his center sees the center of life, its goal: the place where all things become new and transform us.

A text therefore begins to live and to act when it finds a heart which beats in unison with it. This reading is then itself a way: that of the spiral which slowly penetrates into the depths and leads us from one level of consciousness to another. This path is not *knowing* but *being*; the maturity which is a rebirth in our very core, there where the word is Presence beyond all reading.

Alphonse and Rachel Goettmann

CHAPTER I

THE CALL OF SILENCE

The world has forgotten silence. Yet it is in silence that the world has its origin and its end. God is also silence and, since we are in His image, the depth of our being is silence. This explains the rise of anguish and fear of death at the heart of the noise which reigns in the cities and now reaches the most distant countryside and the last corners of our forests. Technology in its varied forms never ceases to invade everything and slows down for nothing. Tormented by the unconquerable yearning for our original silence, people of our time are beginning to escape into the deserts, in the retreats of monasteries or in exotic vacations, the symbols of a lost world. Faced with this general asphyxiation, it is important to have these breaths of fresh air in order to survive in the short term. But in the long term, we must learn to live fully in each moment and not only during certain spiritual experiences. The desert is our own being and our heart is a monastic cell, for the beyond is within our depths. There, in the very midst of the noise, is found plenitude.

Yet in order to take this path, we must first learn about it. This requires an education in both humanity and God who meet each other only in the common language of silence. There is an alphabet and a grammar of silence. If we study it, if we daily spell out its reality, its mystery awakens within us and immerses us in its presence. There is a culture of silence: it is a manner of being which is acquired through practice. The aim is to make efforts which eventually lead to a permanent state. We first "do" exercises, then we *become* exercise; we say prayers but we must eventually *become* prayer; we go to the liturgy but our whole being is called to become liturgical and daily life is meant to be a celebration; we seek to experience God, but in doing so we ourselves become gods! That is why Saint Seraphim of Sarov (1759-1833) says: "No spiritual exercise is as good as that of silence." The role of the Tradition and of the Church is to constantly immerse us into this wisdom and give us the means to accomplish it.

THE SILENCE OF THE PASSIONS

The first of all the means is the clear gaze upon oneself which allows us to discern the opposite of inner silence and its great obstacle: the noisy tumult of the passions. When we are cut off from God, we do not live in our spirit, where silence dwells, but in our soul (our psyche), which is in duality. Instead of living through God, of seeing everything in His light and with His eyes, the soul sees and lives through itself in an autonomous way. This is the false self, non-being which no longer feeling the unique inner desire for God, feeds the multiple external desires born from this separation. We seek to satisfy this absolute thirst in the relative (the material), and attach ourselves infinitely to the finite.

Soon, all relationships are falsified: with oneself, with others, with God, with the whole of creation. This profound denaturation engenders in us a predisposition to misdirected faith, through which we always seek to make things other then what they are so that they may satisfy in every moment our appetite for pleasure, power, and

23

arbitrary impulse. Our existence is fractured and pushes us endlessly into internal contradictions.

Where does our pleasure come from and where is it going? This is the realm of asceticism, its primary focus and the very location where conversion occurs. This is a watchfulness of every internal and external movement. Nothing is possible, no accomplishment, no happiness, no peace, as long as desire is turned in upon itself, egocentric and greedy! The Fathers unanimously agree that no spiritual path and no prayer is feasible without battle with these passionate desires; love itself can only be born when the self renounces its position of absolute autonomy.

Confronted with the multiplicity of our desires, the most important step is for each of us to discover our greatest weakness. It is impossible to do battle on all fronts, but it is vital to struggle with one issue at a time. Christ proposes a method which allows us to discover it: what is my primary inclination where my preferences and aspirations are ceaselessly directed? **"For where your treasure is, there your heart will be also."** (Matt. 6:21) Everyone has their Isaac, their unique attachment which they are invited to sacrifice. There is no liberation nor wisdom without silencing that which cries the loudest within us.

FASTING: A FOUNDATIONAL EXPERIENCE

Fasting is the radical means to cut the "wings of desire." It clears the boards and abruptly places us before the evidence of our inclinations. No longer nourishing them from the outside, we become the subject of an ancient revelation within: all our desires are but noise and lies; in reality, we are hungry not for bread but for God. Here fasting reveals its deep mystery: ultimately, all of our desires are inhabited by the unique desire for God. Fasting exposes this desire and when we come off the fast, the conscious satisfaction of any desire becomes in this light a communion with God. That is why the meal is always a eucharist, a communion with the Creator through the creatures who are on the table, for the whole world is the table of a universal banquet offered to humanity in order to assimilate God.

But if we do not do it with this intention, we fall into passions. The state of hunger shows us in what dependence we usually live. If we choose to commune with God through terrestrial foods, we become free and independent and the little ephemeral pleasures become eucharistic joy. We open ourselves through fasting to the life of the spirit, to continual thanksgiving, for everything is a gift of God. That is why fasting never occurs without prayer. The alliance of the two not only chases out the most resistant demons, but leads to a profound transformation of the entire person.

We need to rediscover the weekly twenty-four hour fasting of the first Christians, from Thursday night to Friday night; also the fasting of Advent and Lent, along with those which are in rhythm with the feasts and the seasons. And let us not forget that the time saved during meals belongs to prayer, and the money saved belongs to the poor. "Fasting-Prayer-Alms" is the inseparable triad which restores the body, the soul and the spirit.

LISTENING: THE FUNDAMENTAL ATTITUDE OF THE DISCIPLE

It is at the heart of his fast of forty days that the Christ gives us the secret of this reversal: **"Man shall not live by bread alone, but by every word that proceeds from the**

mouth of God" (Mt 4:4). This is the fundamental habit of the disciple: listening. His whole being is an ear because is whole being is obedience (from the Latin *ob-audire:* to listen). "Hear, O Israel!" is the underlying framework of the whole Bible through which God both gives Himself and provides the method for opening ourselves to this gift. Indeed, the one who has truly practiced listening knows to what extent he is at that moment disconnected from all parasites, for everything is stilled, even distraction and multiple thoughts. At the same time he is plunged into an absymal silence which brings him in touch with the mystery of a Presence. It is for this reason that hearing is the most exercised sense on the path of transformation.

Listening should be permanent since God speaks to us in each moment through the events, encounters and all that occurs within or outside of us. But to recognize His voice on the outside, we must first learn to recognize it within: this is the act of listening to the Word in the Bible. There it is announced by the prophets and is incarnated in Jesus Christ. In contemplating Jesus, in letting ourselves be penetrated by His presence and His word, we are little by little penetrated by the ways of God.

The entire Bible is a real presence of Christ. It is not an ancient text to be read with the intellect but a matter of receiving the Word in communion: the Word assimilates us and we assimilate it. As Origen (2nd century) observed, the reading of the Bible is not added to life, but transforms daily life which becomes the place where the Word speaks ceaselessly. Listening is therefore an exercise of constant vigilance where the right attitude is to commune with the present moment, to become one with that which is here and now because it expresses the will of God; and what God wants is always that which is best for us. Since "everything is grace," even that which is contrary to our wishes, we can "give thanks in all times and places!" This incessant listening to life creates within and around us a prodigious silence—a backdrop of peace, joy and love. This is a continual revelation of God.

MEDITATION: A LOVE STORY

Silent meditation is the indispensable axis of a life which seeks to reach the depths of understanding. It is the commandment of Christ: **"When you pray, go into your room and shut your door"** (Mt 6:6) and the whole

Tradition is filled with this interior consciousness. Along with the Tradition, we take the word "meditation" not in the medieval meaning of reflecting on a religious theme, but in its etymological sense: *itari in medio*, to be led toward the center, the center being the human heart, the throne of God.

Saint Macarius (fifth century) stated that "the heart is the deepest body in the body." We inevitably pray with our body, since it is there, but we do it poorly and with a lack of consciousness. God has taken a body to experience humanity and by living fully in our body, we can experience God! My body is therefore a dazzling path, a sacrament of the One who incarnated Himself in it. We hardly dare to believe the words of Saint John Chrysostom (fourth century): "My body is truly, effectively that of Christ, and not only through faith"; nevertheless, this is the very realism of the eucharist. Gregory Palamas (fourteenth century) cries out: "Flesh of my flesh!"

We must first learn to sit in silence and complete immobility, knowing how to rest corporally in oneself and in God: simply being here, conscious of one's body, feeling it from within, inhabiting it. Breathing will then lead us to the silence of Being, for nothing is more intimate to God and to us than breath. My whole being breathes, I am breathed in . . . Feel this consciously, let yourself be seized by it. Especially, do not breathe voluntarily, let it occur by itself. At each inhalation "God breathes into my nostrils the breath of life" (Gen 2:7), at each exhalation we open ourselves to this Presence, we relax our tensions and surrender ourselves like the clay in the hands of the potter. It is with all His love that God breathes me in. I receive Him with gratitude and remain in this reciprocity of breath where everything is receptivity and gift, in the very image of that which occurs at the heart of the Divine Trinity. Nothing comes out of reflection, especially not God, for everything is in experiential and conscious feeling where, as the Fathers say, the "sensation of the Divine" is found.

THE PRAYER OF JESUS

It is not easy to come out of the multiple and unify oneself around an axis. That is why the Tradition recognizes in the "Prayer of Jesus" one of the greatest means to achieve this. Simple and accessible to everyone, it is repeated as a mantra, either in meditative sitting or in all times and places, inserting itself into the fabric of our daily life: "Lord Jesus Christ, Son of God, have mercy upon me, a sinner." The repetition is done slowly, in peace, without seeking emotion, but with love and adoration. To say each word facilitates from the beginning the union of the intellect with the heart. There are nevertheless great stages which must be gone through over years of practice, from the repetition of the prayer on the lips to the setting ablaze of the heart through grace.

Before beginning the invocation, it is important to ask the help of the Holy Spirit, for "no one can say that Jesus is Lord except by the Holy Spirit." (1 Cor 12:3). Besides, the ground of this Prayer is the ecclesial life with its sacraments and asceticism. Outside of them it cannot take root, anymore than a flower which is torn out of its soil. It is indeed a profession of faith, far beyond an incomprehensible mantra. It engages the whole of our being and structures its depths.

The power of the Name is such that it provokes the real Presence of Christ. His Presence penetrates us, fills us, imbibes us, just as the oil stain silently expands on paper to render it transparent. The Person of Jesus literally fades onto us and modifies us in our smallest detail. By repeating the Name, He ultimately enters into us. His manners, His reactions, His thoughts become ours through a sort of osmosis. Little by little, our life finds itself radically changed. We become resurrected ones, and nothing of our daily life escapes this new orientation. It is as though everything is magnetized by this Name which progressively beats to the rhythm of our heart.

LITURGY: THAT WE MIGHT BECOME GOD

This incredible transformation is a eucharist. As the bread and wine, which are our extended body, become the body and blood of Christ, so is it for the one who prays. It is there, in the liturgy, that all prayer finds both its continual source and the summit of its expression. For it is not a matter of participating once in a while in a liturgy, but rather that our whole being become liturgical and our daily life a celebration, a cosmic liturgy of which we are the priest through all that we do. From this alone will come a new humanity—the Body of Christ—and the transfiguration of the world. But the incandescent hearth of this universal eucharist will always remain the human heart.

When the deacon sings at the beginning of a certain liturgy: "Rise, let us be attentive, in silence!" it is to tear us away from the spirit of the world and the wrong motives of its ideology that makes of us the measure of all things and leads us to believe that happiness is only found in economics, politics, or psychology. The world was not created to be exploited and delivered over to everyone's whims, where humanity finds itself reduced to the slavery we know so well.

The liturgy initiates us into another knowledge: human beings are priests, standing at the center of creation which we receive from the hands of God and which we offer to Him in thanksgiving. The world is therefore the primal matter for the eucharist, which transforms our life in each moment into a life in God. Everything is made in order to commune with God, and work itself is a sacrament. Since nothing has life without God, everything receives meaning or value from offering it to Him in love. This is our daily food, our uninterrupted eucharist, the sacrament of our Joy. For God did not create the universe out of need, but so that His creatures could participate in His joy.

CHAPTER II

THE BOOK OF OUR DESTINY

How many persons have aspired to read the Bible only to find the task impossible and to put it aside in disappointment? Whatever hope they may have had to discover this mysterious and unknown realm has been lost to indifference and emptiness, along with an incapacity to move any further into the reading. Where does this strange resistance come from? Could such a "trial" already be a communication with the Word of Life? We do not enter into the Bible as we might with any other book. How then do we go through this trial that meets us from the onset and that may prove in the end to be salvific?

THE BIBLE: A REAL PRESENCE

The Bible is first of all an open sky: here we learn that God

35

speaks of Himself, of humanity and of our destiny. Here
we learn how we were born and for what purpose, the
reason for our suffering and the great joy which is
promised to us. We discover, beyond all the absurdities,
that life has meaning, that we are loved by a great love, that
God has only one desire: to offer Himself to us, here and
now, in a liberating experience that utterly transforms and
makes new creatures of us.

The Bible is where we find our Source. It is not a book
or a document, but our "Revelation": the Word which
creates us in this moment, which maintains us in existence
at each instant and shapes us toward an always new future.

But there is infinitely more: as we listen, as our whole
being becomes a receptive cup, this Word is made living
and reveals itself as an always present Companion. It is
Someone. The relation which is established with the Bible
is not at all that of subject and object, of the reader and the
book, but a relation of love, of an "I" and a "You," whose
communion will some day bring forth a wedding. That is
the meaning of the "Covenant," which is the true name of
the Bible and its entire fabric. From then on, each
"reading" of the Bible is in fact an invitation to experience:

"Come and See" (John 1:39).

This intimate "listening" as the fundamental attitude of the encounter with God will also allow us to "see" Him everywhere, for the "heavens tell the glory of God and the firmament proclaims the work of His hands" (Ps 19:2); nature will then always be considered as a second Bible. The five senses can maintain a permanent contact with God, as "windows open onto the Invisible," according to the expression of the Fathers. Our senses are the location of the prodigious realism of this experience.

We will not be surprised, then, to see the Bible treated as a sacrament, a real Presence. For the Fathers, the Bible is the Christ. It is not found on library shelves along with all the other books; it has its place on the altar of icons where a candle is permanently lit. There believers can see it, touch it, kiss it, listen to it, enter into dialogue with it. Just like the priest or the deacon during liturgy: the first thing they do when they approach the holy table where lies the Bible is to kiss it and say to it: "Hail, Word of eternal Life!" And the public reading is always done in song for the singing voice comes from somewhere else, beyond a psychic tonality, transmitting the profound vibration of being and making the listener enter into the same resonance. The Tradition reminds us that it is the Christ whom we are hearing. It is an experiential "reading" through which we seek to "taste" the Presence as in the Eucharist and to "smell" His perfume thanks to the incense which surrounds the text. Everything is carnal in this approach, the body is fully involved, as it should be in a reciprocity of love. This is the very logic of the incarnation.

In this copenetration, the Word acts with power, for it is clothed in the very power of God and carries His power: it fertilizes us, molds us and makes a new birth germinate within us. This is made clear from the very first words of the Bible: "God spoke and all was done" (Gn 1). It is in the Word of God that "in Him we live and move and have our being" (Ac 17:28). God himself makes us understand this through the prophet Isaiah: "For as the rain and the snow come down from heaven, and return not thither but water the earth, making it bring forth and sprout, giving seed to the sower and bread to the eater, so shall the word be that goes forth from my mouth; it shall not return to me empty, but it shall accomplish that which I purpose, and prosper in the thing for which I sent it" (Is 55:10-11).

The Word is the creative depth at work in all things. "For the word of God is living and active, sharper than any two-edged sword, piercing to the division of soul and spirit, of joints and marrow, and discerning the thoughts and intentions of the heart" (He 4:12).

The Word is creative power, but also power of restoration for it can save and heal us. It fights the passions and offers itself to us as a marvelous instrument for spiritual progress, a remedy against all ills, far superior to all others. Origen pleaded its cause in the second century and Saint Benedict (sixth century) taught it in his *Rules* to the monks. "He who ignores the Scriptures," said Saint Jerome (fifth century), "ignores the power of God and the wisdom of God, for the ignorance of Scriptures is the ignorance of Christ" (*Commentaries on Isaiah*).

POWER AND WISDOM

Indeed, Jesus Christ is present from one end of the Bible to the other, for this is the "Wisdom" of which it is full. But if

He is present and the Word is living it is because the Spirit rests within it as the Christ himself revealed during his first sermon in Nazareth: **"the Spirit of the Lord is upon Me"** (Lk 4:18), and this is the whole "power" of the Bible. Through it alone, the Christ is revealed to us in every passage of Scripture, and there is not a single jot in which he is not present because the smallest sign unveils something of His face. Neither historical research nor any exegesis can allow us to penetrate into this mysterious Center toward which the whole Bible converges: that place where each word finds its fullness, with the help of the Spirit.

It is on the day of Pentecost that Peter, a man with neither instruction nor culture, but "filled with the Holy Spirit," unveils this new interpretation of scripture to all, to the ancients and the scribes, the pharisees, high priests and other specialists studying the Bible "day and night" by applying it all at once to the whole of Scripture! (Ac 2 to 4)

All that it contains, all its "hows" and "whys," all its promises, every line is fulfilled, actualized and alive in the person of Jesus resurrected. What astonishing boldness that an uneducated man should give the final word on the secular interpretation of Scripture. It could only be the work of the Spirit! From then on it is impossible to fully understand the Bible without seeing, hearing, touching, tasting, smelling within every word Jesus-Christ who is its Presence and accomplishment.

That is why we can say that there is no "Old" Testament but rather a real Presence of Christ which is always new until His definitive advent. In the Sermon on the Mount, Jesus Himself reveals this as the true meaning and outcome of the Scriptures: **"It was said to those of old . . . but I say to you . . . "**(Mt 5:21). To His disciples on the road to Emmaus, "He expounded to them in all the scriptures the things concerning Himself." (Lk 24:27). Jesus' entire mission takes up the very depth of the Hebrew Text to bring to completion the adventure begun with Israel and to fulfill the writing of all the prophets. What an overwhelming sign of continuity it is in the will of Jesus to choose twelve disciples to follow the twelve tribes of Israel and to preside over the destinies of the Church, the new Israel!

It is no surprise then to find the New Testament full of quotes from the Old Testament, along with its tension and

41

its spirit. The two Testaments interpenetrate each other and can only be understood through a reciprocal reading. We can have access to the Old Testament only through the eyes and heart of the New one, reading everything in the light of its accomplishment through the Christ; and inversely, the one who is familiar with the Jewish roots of our faith will know Christ from within by His genealogy and the stages of His coming among us; the New Testament will appear to him as the explosion of "Good News."

This has nothing to do with an objective study that is external to us. The Old Testament lives within us, it describes the stages of our own spiritual growth. The faith and long hope of our ancestors—the patriarchs and the prophets—are inscribed in the depths of our being.

Without Jesus Christ nothing would exist of this immense history. He was the Word of God before His incarnation, all that is contained in the Old Testament was His work and His word, all that is described in the Scriptures was done by Him. He called Abraham toward his new destiny, He sent Moses on his grandiose mission, He led the Hebrews toward the Promised Land and gave them drink in the desert. He is the rock from which surges the living waters (1 Co 10:4) and the bread that falls from the sky, He is Himself the Law in person and the word which comes out of the mouth of prophets, He is already "the heart of flesh" of the righteous evoked by Ezekiel (36:26).

Thus the great witnesses of the Old Testament whom we call "prefigurations" of Christ are less an annunciation of Christ as they are a veiled Presence. This is the same relationship as between the seed and the ear of corn: the real contents of the cob are already present in the seed, as are the prefigurations of Christ in the Old Testament. It is Christ who suffers in Job and with Job, for Christ is present in every verse of the book of Job. Only the suffering and death of Christ on the cross, His surrender into the hands of the Father explain the story of Job as a stage toward the passion of Jesus which is the culmination of a process already at work since the fall of humanity!

We could say the same concerning Isaac offered in sacrifice, of David the Messianic King, of the Lamb led to slaughter, of the Good Shepherd or the Suffering Servant, of the martyrdom of Jeremiah, etc. So many extraordinary portraits of Christ rise up in these texts as though His face wanted to break through the veil of appearances that still hides it. We could cite all of Isaiah, then each of the prophets, peel the least verse of the Psalms and immerse ourselves entirely in the Song of Songs. At first the reader will be seized with amazement by certain revelations, then as the gaze becomes contemplative and the heart full of love, he will see the presence of Christ everywhere and perhaps also in the great silences that some words leave behind them, in the unspoken for the essential ultimately escapes all formulation. It is in these silences that the Word speaks loudest.

THE BOOK OF OUR TRANSFORMATION

The Word of God is alive because it is the living Christ. But as a word, it has the virtue of being able to penetrate us as a seed penetrates the earth, and there it germinates and develops in our depths as new life which will illuminate our whole being from within (Ps 118:105) and conform us to Christ himself: "having been born again, not of corruptible seed but incorruptible, through the word of God which lives and abides forever" (1 Pet 1:23).

The etymological meaning of "word" (*dabar* in Hebrew) is the depth of things, that which is hidden and which the word will reveal. It therefore awakens us to our identity and our true vocation, just as it carries all things in the universe to their ultimate fulfillment. This is the Jewish vision of the word, an acting and efficient power, a voice that manifests a presence, a desire for communion. Our intellectual approach to the Word, according to the Greek conception which seeks a knowledge about God, is an attitude which objectifies and keeps things at a distance. We can know the Word, be a fount of science concerning it, and yet have never encountered it.

That is why we cannot undergo an apprenticeship of an authentic reading except in the Church. We are not referring to the socio-political structure, but to the plenitude of wisdom that it possesses and that alone can understand the plenitude of wisdom which is the Bible. The Spirit goes where it wills, but it has chosen to place itself fully only in the Church. Yet it is the Spirit that has dictated the Scriptures and through its unction, the Spirit rests on every baptized person, as it rests in the Word, and gives that person the faculty to read it as priest, king, and prophet. This is always an ecclesiastical reading, even if it occurs in the solitude of one's room.

The reader is inspired as a prophet and finds himself on the same wavelength as the text itself. We are given the prophetic grace of a radically new understanding of history, we are taken beyond a simple narrative or literal reading and placed there where things originate. Inspired, we can receive from the text a message which is not in the text and that will remain inexhaustible.

As king, the reader is called to realize the received word in history. First it must be fulfilled in his personal life: the Word sanctifies him, orients his being, His royalty overcomes the empire of the passions and tears him away from the kingdom of darkness. This transformation of his heart is also the incandescent hearth of all transformation in the world. As king, He consecrates history which becomes sacred history, the history of our liberation. Because it is prophetic, the reading becomes a political act where we enter with God into the same covenant.

As priest, his reading is a liturgical act where the synchronicity between the event related in the Bible and our current experience is revealed. The Word is absolutely present for him: it is now that the event read in the Bible is realized. If this is not the case, the Word is not divine and does not transcend time. For the liturgy does not celebrate a memorial from the past: it is here and now that Jesus dies and is resurrected! In fact, Jesus Himself gives us this way of interpreting Scripture when one day He read in the synagogue the passage from Isaiah 61, some several centuries old, and told His stunned listeners: **"Today this Scripture is fulfilled in your hearing"** (Lk 4:21). Later He stated: **"Heaven and earth will pass away, but My words will by no means pass away"** (Mt 24:35).

THE CONDITIONS OF A FRUITFUL READING

1. THE INVOCATION OF THE HOLY SPIRIT

Obviously, prayer is the preamble of the process. Just as the eucharistic bread and wine presuppose the *epiclesis* (the invocation of the Holy Spirit), in order to become the living presence of Christ, so the Word comes alive for us through this same invocation of the Spirit that rests within it. The whole Tradition teaches that as soon as we receive the Word in prayer, the Spirit makes it internal and communicates its experience to us. It makes a sacrament of the Word which becomes flesh within us. But without the invocation of the Spirit, nothing will take place; the text will only be a relic from a concluded past, with no more interest than the writings of ancient philosophers.

2. A SET RENDEZVOUS

After prayer comes the time of the reading itself. William de Saint-Thierry (thirteenth century) tells us in his *Golden Letter:* "At set hours, we must give ourselves to a specific reading. A reading found by accident, with no direction, far from edifying the soul, throws it into inconstancy." It is important to set both the time of our reading and its length. This discipline is part of the necessary asceticism and already opens the heart to the gift of self. If the Bible is truly a Presence for us, then this time will be a rendezvous. Who would dare miss it? And recollecting in a secret place is indispensable.

3. A CHOSEN TEXT

It is careless to open the Bible halfheartedly or flip

through it according to our whims. Such a reading will bear no fruit. It is true that in times of great decisions, when what is at stake is the crossing over to a new stage of our life or a great turning point, we can, after long prayer, open the Bible and put our finger on the text that will truly be a help from heaven. Many saints have done this, but this remains the exception.

There must be a method to the daily study of Scripture. Following a liturgical calendar is an excellent one; it allows us to be in communion with the great mysteries that are unfolding during the year and that forge our consciousness with the Church. Besides, placing in parallel the texts of the Old and New Testaments shows their profound inner unity.

Another way consists in simply reading the New Testament from beginning to end, a little every day, and starting over indefinitely. From the Old Testament, the Psalms should be our daily bread because this is praying with the very words of the Holy Spirit. For the rest, it will probably be easier to begin with the prophets, then Isaiah to Malachy, then the books for edification such Toby, Job, the Song of Songs, etc., and only then the historical books.

There also exists among certain publishers methods that make it possible to read the Bible throughout the year, paralleling the two Testaments. Whoever says that they do not have time could take just one verse per day and carry it with him, pondering it all day long. Saint Teresa de Lisieux used to say: "I take a verse of Scripture as a chicken takes a drop of water: she raises her beek and lets it descend slowly." This suggests that the Bible always remains open and that we take the verses chronologically.

We will also come across obscure passages which we will not understand or which will leave us indifferent, but this is of no importance, for who understands the Eucharist? The important thing is to commune with the Word as we do with the body and blood of Christ. We received the text as it comes, for itself, without seeking anything for oneself through emotional satisfaction. Heidegger would say: "Rather than to understand, we must let ourselves be taken." The Word takes root within us, creates a path and, transforming us from within, will give us little by little an understanding which is not merely mental and which will progressively illuminate the texts with the very light of God. The Fathers tell us that it is only in becoming Christ oneself that we truly understand the Scriptures.

4. TAKING THE TIME TO SAVOR A TEXT

The preceding leads us to the quality of the reading. We must know how to stop, then read and reread the text over and over again for a long time in order to savor it. Saint Gregory the Great (sixth century) speaks of the "rumination" and of "mastication" of the Word until "our stomach contains the book and our entrails are full of it." This idea is also found in Ezechiel 10:1-11 and throughout the Jewish Tradition (see Psalm 118). This was the practice of all the Fathers: the Word must penetrate the spirit, the soul and the body; this impregnation gave birth in them to an incessant meditation: they assimilated the Scriptures and the Scriptures assimilated them.

This suggests a great perseverance in reading. Such an effort is truly the sign and the measure of our spiritual progress, for it expresses our hunger and thirst for the Word. Our many desires find a response there in the unique desire for God. Saint Jerome wrote that "perseverance engenders familiarity." Without regularity, nothing can take place in any area of endeavor: "In perseverance will you find your crowning" (Rev 2:10). Long and frequent study of the Bible opens us to its spirit, its language, its forms of expressions, the fundamental attitudes which it suggests, and will end by envangelizing us right into our reflexes, even the unconscious ones, unveiling secret and hidden things to us. This is an immersion in the Word where we become one with it.

Finally, the unique effort that is asked of us is to remain in the Word: **"If you abide in My Word, you are my disciples indeed, and you shall know the truth,"** said the Christ (John 8:31). To remain in the Word is to remain with Christ, this is what we are called and chosen to do before all things. And this is also the answer that Christ himself gives to us, that we might seek where He is staying (John 1:38-39).

We can say more: to return again and again to the texts that have touched the secret fiber of our being is to respond to a particular call in which the Spirit gives each of us a sign. Everyone will then have his or her texts in the Bible, marked in red, and known by heart, for when we come into contact with them they warm the heart. These starry moments signify a letting go of the unilateral supremacy of the soul, that is, of the ego or the psyche, and the opening of the heart-spirit, the throne of Grace, where "the Spirit Himself makes intercession for us with groanings which cannot be uttered" (Rom 8:26). The experience is indescribable as is all intimate encounter, but these manifestations always result in "peace, joy and love," the fruits of the spirit, the signs that we have descended into the heart, there where the immediate contact with God takes place and where we hear the voice of the Beloved through such a word. Then we come into silence, into a contemplative state. This culmination of the prayerful approach to the Bible is always trinitarian: Silence-Source which is the Father; the Word which is Christ; Unction-Joy-groaning of the Spirit. Every Word of the Bible rises out of the abyss of Silence and returns toward an abyss of Silence, coming to us through the power of the Spirit.

This is far from mere reading. The Word truly acts as the Eucharist; we receive a Presence, it is a matter of communion. The whole Tradition speaks of "two tables of the Lord": the liturgy and the Word which is also "bread of Christ, flesh of the lamb, His Body and Blood" (Saint

Jerome). Origen tells us that we "eucharistically consume the Word which has been mysteriously broken," and to go from the table of the written Word to the table of the transubstantial Word undoubtedly makes possible the best reading of the Bible. We know well only that which we have in our body and blood! The transmission of meaning is also a transmission of blood, a knowledge through connaturality and transformation from one to the other. Therefore, to read is equivalent to eating the Word. The purpose of the Word is to incorporate itself into the one who listens and submits himself to it. We are by nature "mimers" who repeat in inner micro-gestures the words that we receive. The vibration penetrates into the body and structures it, models it in our psychosomatic being through "miming." That is why we are invited, both in the Old and New Testament to eat the book and fill ourselves (Ez 3:3 - Rev: 10:9).

As with the eucharistic communion, we become the Word, we assimilate it as all other food, because we become what we eat: the Word is made flesh in us, there is a co-corporality with it. Cabasilas (fifteenth century) says that "the blood from which we live is actually the Blood of

Christ, and the flesh which inserts the sacrament into us is the Body of Christ."

Is this not the ultimate and complete meaning of the word "conversion"? The Word of God "converts" itself in us, in the etymological meaning of the word, and becomes our substance which is transformed through the action of this interiorized power.

PUTTING THE WORD IN PRACTICE

The Holy Scriptures purify our passions and burn the obstacles on this path only with our cooperation. As with the Burning Bush, they invite us to take off the sandals of our ego (Ex 3:5). This is the work of asceticism and of the holiness of life which puts the Word of God into practice. Only a pure heart becomes a receptive cup and allows the penetration of Scripture into our depths.

It goes without saying that this is a reciprocity of love between God and human beings. In this living relationship with the Bible, we will not seek an increase in knowledge, or a study of God, but only the reading of God, coming to know Him by being born into His mystery. This way of approaching the text has its own inherent asceticism: perseverance, continuity, silence, recollection, and only then transformation. Our whole being is engaged and focused, leading us into a new way of life.

Origen tells us that "the more we make daily progress in the reading of Scripture and the deeper the mind goes into it, the more we are renewed every day." All life progressively unifies itself around the Word of God; according to the beautiful image given by Saint John Cassian (fourth century), our life is carried by the Bible as a boat is carried by the waves of the sea. Our roots are fixed in God. Just as a sailor on his ship far at sea sees only the ocean, so the one who reads, re-reads, assimilates and ruminates Scripture sees only God in everything and everywhere: he or she has become a contemplative. As Origen observes, the reading of the Bible is not added to life, but transforms daily life into a living reading of the Word, and life becomes the place where the Word speaks ceaselessly. It is this practice which is our heritage. Our Fathers lived the Bible, thought and spoke through it, until they had identified themselves with the Word itself. And this is not only the practice of monks! According to Saint

John Chrysostom (fourth century), the reading of the Scriptures is the priestly work of the laity which leads them to saintliness: "This is much more necessary to you who are in the midst of the world than it is to monks," says Origen. "There is worse than not reading Scripture, and that is to believe that Scripture is useless, for this is truly ignorance." The "In Trullo" Council (tenth century) tells priests to initiate the believers into a greater intimacy with the Bible. Even children must develop the habit of an attentive and daily reading of Scripture. The birth of the inner person takes years, and we only truly become such by being born into the spiritual life. We can see then the exclusive and irreplaceable role of the Word of God throughout our life as a path of continual rebirth toward deification. We become a person only by becoming god. And it is the Word of God which pulls us up from nothingness into being, and in each moment creates us and gives us life. It is from the Word alone that we will some day enter into supreme happiness.

All those who are familiar with the Word know, as did our Fathers in the faith, moments of amazing ravishment in which we feel ourselves overflowing with love for the Lord and our whole being begins to dance. David, drunk with joy, danced around the Ark containing the Word of God; the prophets, seized by the Word which they were to transmit, found themselves caught up in such ecstasies of joy; John the Baptist, the annunciator of the Word made flesh, already danced with joy in the stomach of his mother, and Mary, pregnant with the Word, danced the Magnificat.

"My soul magnifies the Lord and my spirit rejoices in God my Savior!"

CHAPTER III

THE SURPRISING PRACTICE OF PRAISE

The books of the American pastor Merlin Carothers have sold over six million copies and thousands of readers have written to the author testifying to their fabulous adventure: "Praise is spiritual dynamite possessing an explosive power. It revolutionizes all that it comes in contact with. For it is our point of contact with God." (Carothers, *The Power of Praise*).

Could this not be the beginning of a radically new life? Did Jesus not say: **"If you have faith and do not doubt, you will not only do what was done to this fig tree, but also if you say to this mountain, 'Be removed and be cast into the sea,' it will be done"** (Mt 21:21). In other words: "With God nothing will be impossible!" (Lk 1:37), and all the miracles are very little to Him who by the power at work within us is able to do far more abundantly than all that we ask or think (Ep 3:20). Jesus gives sight to the blind, the deaf hear, the paralyzed walk, the lepers are purified and the dead are resurrected, and He invites us to do the same (Mk 16:17-18). **"Most assuredly I say to you, he who believes in Me, the works that I do he will do also; and greater works than these he will do"** (Jn 14:12). The greatest work of all is, of course, not the healing of a blind or paralyzed person, but the entering as of now into the Kingdom of Heaven, discovering that the Christ brought us a way of being which is utterly different than the world's way. It is called fullness of joy (Jn 15:11; 17:13) and abundance of life (Jn 10:10). To live here and now as resurrected ones and to be life's witnesses is our true inheritance.

The lever for this new life and this faith is praise and thanksgiving. Praise is faith in action, the practice of daily life. Bless, for to this you have been called (1 Pt 3:9).

THE AMAZING LOVE OF GOD

Indeed, it is revealed to us in the Bible that God in His great love wants to communicate Himself to us. He creates the universe and all that it contains in order to give Himself. All that exists, without exception, is a gift of God to humanity whom He loves exceedingly. This is not humanity in general, but you personally, for the love of God can only be unique and personal. In other words, in all that exists, not only nature but in space, in the air that we breath, in the time that we live and the events which He directs at each moment, in all this God is present. Through it all He wants to make Himself known to us, courting us like a fiance and seeking to make of our life a communion with Him. This astonishing love, through which God constantly seeks us, is the deep fabric of the whole Bible from the beginnings to the death of Christ on the cross and His resurrection. God loves me to the death. God seeks me, in this moment, here where I am, and through the very instant that I am living he wants to say to me "I love you." The content of this present moment is filled with the best that He wants to give me, whatever my ego may think of it.

Only a loving God could have deposited in our depths this inextinguishable hunger within us. For we are "in the image of God": if God is love, humanity is love and God is hungry for us, which explains why we are inhabited by such hunger! And that is also why we never stop eating. We eat constantly with our five senses; with the mouth of course, but also with the eyes, the ears, the touch, the heart and the mind. We must eat to live and we see in the Bible that the whole world is offered as the table of a universal banquet, from creation to the eschatalogical banquet, the wedding of the Lamb. Jesus himself manifested for the first time His glory at a wedding meal (Jn 2:1-12) and continually compares the Kingdom of God to a feast. To be is to eat, because to eat consciously is to commune with God; to receive each moment as a gift of God is to assimilate it, making it our flesh and blood. We become what we eat and for humanity to eat is to become god, to divinize oneself. This is the whole story of this love between God and humanity, which culminates in the eucharistic meal where daily life finally finds its transfiguration.

To discover this experientially is unquestionably the most important turning point of our life. I am a being who is hungry, but in reality it is a hunger for God; I am filled with desires, but in their depths is found the unique desire for God! The loss of this consciousness is the fall of humanity which occurs every day of our lives in our separation from the loving intention of God. To eat is then no longer an uninterrupted communion with Him, but rather a taking of things as an end in themselves, loving them for themselves rather than because God is present within them. Without God, things do not contain Life, and are incapable in and of themselves to nourish our hunger for eternity. This is the hell of the emptiness of daily life, because we commune with death in each moment and make a cemetery of the world.

THE MEANING OF THE PRESENT MOMENT

To recognize that everything is a gift from God, that at each moment His love offers itself to our hunger and seeks to fill us, opens in and around us a true paradise of new life and joy which were heretofore entirely unknown! We discover that we are born for gratitude, praise, benediction. "Bless, for that is what you were called to do," said Saint Peter. This jubilation of consciousness is the whole Way, a highway which goes straight to the heart of human beings and to the heart of God which is their place of contact. This is not one possibility among others, but our vocation: in the Bible, to bless God is the only way to live, and not to do so is to die. This is the great secret of happiness, that of God himself. For we need only open the first pages of Genesis to see that God manifests himself by blessing: God blesses all that He has done, that is, He fills all creation with His presence and His love. And when God asks humanity to give a name to things (Gn 2:19), He is asking us to bless in turn that with which we come in contact.

In the Bible, to give a name does not mean to distinguish one thing from the other or to classify it in a mental category. To do so is precisely a consequence of our fall and a relationship to death. Among the ancient Hebrews (the *shem*), a name contained the secret nature of every being; it referred to its emanation. "To name," in the semitic mentality, is to *know* fully, there where a thing is "born" and finds its Source. This ultimately means recognizing the face of God in everything. The name reveals the essence of a thing as gift of God, containing His Presence and opening it to joy, benediction, gratitude.

He who names in this faith lifts the veil of appearances to encounter and reach in every moment the depth of things. His consciousness is illumined by grace and apprehends the transparence of all that surrounds him; this is a transfiguration in the full meaning of the word: he sees the true Figure of reality. That is why the pious Jew whose spirit is seeded by this "knowledge" knows how to read in every moment the revelation of the Holy Name under the most ordinary appearances. From morning to night, he blesses everything, because everything is the Burning Bush, that place of fire where Moses learns that God is the incandescent core of all that is (Ex 3). This is a continual amazement, even before the little things. The unique Name is sanctified in all names and the present moment becomes the field of His love. All lovers recognize themselves in this, as they spell out the name of their beloved under all its facets.

We stand therefore at the center of the world as priests: we receive the world from the hands of God and offer it back to God; we receive divine grace through all things and give thanks for everything by blessing it. Our life is a celebration, a "cosmic liturgy" according to the expression of Saint Maximus the Confessor (seventh century), and we transform our life into a Life in God. Our whole being becomes liturgical and what we live here and now, all that we touch and encounter, becomes the material of a universal Eucharist, that is, of thanksgiving. Even that which is contrary or hostile to us contains the seeds of a complete turnabout. To enter into a relation of gratitude and adoration with everything confers upon us the divine power to transform life through praise.

THE OLD TESTAMENT: CLAMORS OF JOY

Even though sin—separation from God—continuously tears us away from our divine condition and, far from being priests of the world, we are often its slaves, the fact remains that admiration before God is the reason for human life. This contemplative gaze, which takes root in our heart and goes to the heart of all things, this immense joy of seeing that God is God, and the praise which is its expression, appear throughout the Old Testament: "I will bless the Lord at all times, His praise shall continually be in my mouth" (Ps 34:1). The Jew tirelessly goes over in his heart the marvels of the history of Israel and of Creation, for as Ecclesiastes states: "Who could tire from contemplating the glory of God?" The Hebrew people live, walk, and breathe only beneath the radiance of this glory, constantly regenerated by His power and illumined by His presence: "Arise, shine; for your light has come, and the glory of the Lord is risen upon you" (Is 60:1).

The Jewish soul could let itself be seized with wonder and explode with joyous gratitude through praise and thanksgiving. At the feasts of Israel and during the worship of the Temple, they sang, beat their hands, cried out in exclamations of enthusiastic joy with clamors to shake the earth. The feasts and celebrations lasted for days, the liturgical joy of the people was overwhelming, as though they were seeking to make this cry take root forever in the depths of being: "For eternal is His love!" They always sang, even on the darkest days, so that it might resonate on days without feasts. For they knew from experience that, rising out of the living contact with God, praise awakens the whole person (Ps 57:8 or 108:2) and leads us into a renewal of life; it is the great sign, as the philosophers say, that "life triumphs" (Bergson). Indeed, it is not the dead who worship God.

But where does this incredible power of praise come from? Why these constant exhortations to the people to be joyous? Because in the very midst of this joy and jubilation, within the praise itself is revealed the face of God: Give thanks to the Lord, call out His name . . . Sing, play for Him . . . Seek the Lord and His strength, seek His face (Ps 105:1-5; 89:16-17 and especially 22:4). Here we begin to see revealed the great mystery of praise: Joy is a gift of God which makes Him present. When we let it penetrate within, when we vibrate with song and praise, there is a knowledge through this vibration. We become what we sing, and we only know well that which we have in our flesh and blood. All authentic spiritual life is characterized by this wonder, which the ancient Greeks called the instrument of knowledge par excellence. The one who does not live with joy and a song in his heart has not experienced God: this is a universal certainty. That is why all the traditions sing and seek inner exaltation! "And the ransomed of the Lord shall return, and come to Zion with singing; with everlasting joy on their heads; they shall obtain joy and gladness, and sorrow and sighing shall flee away" (Is 35:10).

THE NEW TESTAMENT: THE SOLUTION TO ALL OUR PROBLEMS

Saint Paul says with power that the primary sin of the pagans is that "they did not glorify Him as God nor were thankful . . . for His invisible attributes are clearly seen, being understood by the things that are made" (Rm 1:20-21). What shall be said of the sin of Christians who only see this glory from the outside, but yet are configured to it through the resurrected Christ! Saint Isaac the Syrian (sixth century), this giant of orthodox mysticism, reminds us that there is no greater sin than to be insensitive to the joy of Christ resurrected.

Through Him, God has filled us beyond all measure. "He, who being the brightness of His glory and the express image of His person" (He 1:3), "the glory of God in the face of Jesus Christ" (2Co 4:6), and He comes to assimilate us to Him through the power of the Spirit. We are "co-inheritors" of Christ "for the Spirit searches all things, yes the deep things of God" (1 Co 2:10) and joins himself to us to reveal the secret of this mystery which "eye has not seen, nor ear heard, the things which God has prepared for those who love Him" (1 Co 2:9). This is our life in Christ, for to live in plenitude is to let Christ live within us, an osmosis whose experience greatly surpasses the transfiguration of Moses on Sinai and everything of which the Old Testament, however grandiose, was only the announcement.

Yet the life of Jesus is an incessant thanksgiving in order to lead us with Him into the same movement and open the heavenly dimension of the world for us, resurrecting us to the celestial condition which is none other than praise as Revelation constantly reminds us. Praise and thanksgiving are not only Christ's way of being, but are His very Being. He always gives thanks to God, even in situations which we would consider "impossible" such as the multiplication of bread (Mk 6:41), or "tragic" such as the death of His friend Lazarus (Jn 11:41). Jesus shows us that the loving presence of the Father is behind everything, even that which seems horrible to us; thanksgiving makes it possible to "recognize" Him and liberates the power of the divine action. "For with God nothing will be impossible" (Lk 1:37) and we can be stunned to see that there is never any tragedy around Jesus. With him, the tragedy of life disappears, even at the heart of His own death which he makes a glorification of His Father (Jn 17:1), and death becomes the source of life. That is where, in the supreme gesture of His passion, Christ reveals the profound energy of His being: the immense thanksgiving to the Father which eternally fills the Son's heart! For in descending into the darkest corner of the human condition and in consecrating it to the Father, Christ sanctifies us (Jn 17:19). He liberates us and pulls us out of our hell. This transformation is the very meaning of the Eucharist and in communing with it, with the Body and Blood of Christ, we in turn become thanksgiving and are transformed into a pure "praise of His glory" (Ep 1:12). In Christ, living for Him and He living for us, life becomes a eucharistic sacrament and communion, that is, permanent praise and thanksgiving.

From then on there is a specifically Christian way of living out every problem, every difficulty, every suffering and even death. This way is to unite oneself intimately with Jesus and to give thanks with Him, praising God for all that we live here and now. This is the unique solution! It is entirely irrational and often crucifies our understanding, but there, "nailed on the cross with Christ" and liberated from "the wisdom of the world," we truly experience a secret and mysterious "power" which is that of Christ resurrected and living in us. Here is the foundation of a totally new life and new being. All of existence becomes Paschal: through incessant thanksgiving, we transform life from darkness to light. In each moment life surges out of circumstances of death, just as, in the Eucharist, the bread and wine become Body and Blood of Christ. This is what the Gospel has brought us: the presence of the dazzling beauty of Christ resurrected at the heart of each instant to metamorphosize it into joy! Now "everything is grace"!

LEARN PRAISE AND YOU WILL LEARN GOD

The first Christians were right: "They brought no program, no theory, but everywhere they went the seed of the Kingdom germinated, faith became inflamed, life was transfigured, the impossible became possible, because their whole being was a living torch of praise for the resurrected Christ; He and He alone was the unique joy of their life and the goal of the Church was none other than to make present to the world and to history the joy of the resurrected Christ, in whom all things have their beginning and their end" (A. Schmemann, *For the Life of the World*).

The first Christians made thanksgiving the very fabric of their renewed lives. In reading the New Testament, we are surprised by the abundance of these manifestations, from Zachary's great doxologies (canticles of thanksgiving), to old Symeon and Mary's Magnificat (Lk 1:46-55), to the reflexes of thanksgiving of the Apostles and the first communities, and especially in the extraordinary texts of Saint Paul which show him in continual thanksgiving and inviting others to do the same: "Rejoice always, pray without ceasing, in everything give thanks; for this is the will of God in Christ Jesus for you" (1 Th 5:16-18).

This biblical vein continues down through the tradition of the Fathers. For them, God did not create the universe out of need, but so that the creatures could participate in His joy. We can therefore say that a being without joy is not a sign of the love of God. Saint Basil the Great (fourth century) did not want work accomplished by a monk without praise and filled with muttering to be mixed with the work of others and used for the community! For Saint Theodore the Studious (eighth century) work is a service to God, a liturgy where we celebrate the presence of the Name, that is, of Christ. Saint Benedict (sixth century) stated that we are to look upon "even utensils and broomsticks as though they were sacred vases of the altar." To live is simply "to love God," said Saint Augustine (fifth century) "and to sing His glory, and better yet: to become oneself a song of glory." And one of the very first Fathers, Saint Clement of Alexandria (second century) gave tonality to the whole Christian tradition: "It is not in a specific place, nor in a privileged temple, nor on certain celebrations or chosen days, but in every instant of life, in all places that the perfect Christian proclaims his thanksgiving. Going through our life as in a celebration, certain that God is always everywhere, we sing while we work, we travel to the singing of hymns, we conduct ourselves in everything as citizens of heaven" (*Stromatas 2*).

But this is only possible because at the heart of all things is found liturgy, a veritable bath of divine glory, a feast of feasts, an apprenticeship into an unsuspected life. What celebration it is indeed, for the only obstacle to life—death—is no longer such: "Christ is resurrected, risen from the dead, trampling down death by death and upon those in the tombs bestowing Life!" This refers not only to the final tomb, but to all enclosures and to all prisons which the ego builds daily. "The supreme ill can become supreme joy" is a phrase from a great spiritual person that can send shivers through us (Sertillanges, *On Death*). Has Christ not transformed the tomb into a nuptial chamber (according to the Orthodox Easter liturgy)? The benediction of God rests in all things and those people who are capable of blessing and praising all things give rise to miracles. Saint Isaac the Syrian tells us that "his life, his joy are the Christ, the Light of the Father. Such a person rejoices at all times through the contemplation of his soul, and is amazed by the beauty he sees that is a hundred times more luminous than the solar splendor. This is the Kingdom of God hidden within us. From this consciousness, love is born" (*Spiritual Writings*). This is the condition of the ascetics who are dead to themselves and of those who are filled with the love of God. Joy has divinized them.

ON YOUR MARK

We are part of this lineage of beings on fire, their tradition is ours, for we are baptized with the same Spirit and the same fire (Lk 3:16). That is the secret of our deep being, it is the secret of all things, all events, and of every situation. "Baptism" means to be literally "immersed"; the baptized one is someone who is immersed in Christ and who ceaselessly plunges into his or her own depths in order to keep in contact with Him. He is someone who does not let himself be swept away by external appearances or revolting circumstances, for he also plunges into them to find the Divine Presence. This immersion within everything, done at every moment, is made through continual benediction and nourished by the Eucharist.

The alarm clock goes off in the morning and we already begin to grumble. Let us immediately turn it around and say: "Blessed are You, O Lord, for this new day that You give me!" We risk a glance out the window, and face a minor catastrophe: it's raining! And the usual melancholy seizes us. Is that our only alternative? Try then to repeat: "Alleluia! I say thank You to You, Creator of heaven and earth, for this weather which You make . . . Allelulia! Allelulia!" and repeat it until there is not a trace left of moodiness. It is through the tiny details of each day that we must exercise ourselves: a hurtful statement, a bothersome fly, a barking dog, a stone we step on, a lamp burning out, a car breaking down . . . It is here that is patiently created a new attitude before life right into our reflexes which are never mastered but are now molded by praise. Little by little, "blessed are You, O Lord!" will rise up spontaneously on our lips in relation to everything. We must tirelessly exercise ourselves, always beginning again. This is a true battle, especially when things do not go as we would like.

We learn to *recognize* that we are not masters of our life, but that God is. To praise Him is to give Him the reins, to surrender ourselves to His love with confidence and joy, submitting ourselves to His will in all things. Some days will be more difficult than others, when everything is darkened and God seems absent; we are submerged in suffering or some problem blocks all our horizons. Here praise will not express joy but acceptance with the knowledge that God is at work in spite of everything, if we bless Him. "I do not understand what is happening, Lord, I am weak and overwhelmed, but You know why I must live this; You guide me and You guide each of my steps, I surrender myself into Your hands and I bless You for all things and for each moment. Blessed are You, O lord, may Your holy Name be blessed in everything!"

William Law said: "If someone pretended to show you the shortest and surest way leading to happiness and holiness, he ought to counsel you as a rule of life to thank and praise God for all that happens. For it is certain that, whatever adversity may be encountered, you will transform it into benediction if you praise and thank God for this trial." And Luther wrote: "Happy is he who submits himself to the will of God, for misfortune does not reach him."

CHAPTER IV

THE ICON: TRANSPARENCE
TO BEAUTY

"No one has seen God at any time. The only begotten Son, who is in the bosom of the Father, He has declared Him." (Jn 1:18). The whole history of humanity is balanced on this event: God took on a human face and this face is the privileged expression of His revelation. On this conviction rests the art of the icon which generates such fascination across the centuries. Every person must be able to say with the Apostles: "We have seen the Lord!" (Jn 20:25); thanks to the icon, we can say this today as did the first disciples: "That which was from the beginning . . . which we have seen with our own eyes . . . The Life was manifested, and

79

we have seen, and bear witness." (1 Jn 1:1-2).

THE ICON: THE PLACE WHERE FAITH BECOMES EXPERIENCE

In the Old Testament, Christ manifested himself through the Word, which explains the fundamental attitude of listening which is the fabric of all the Scriptures: "Hear, O Israel!" In the New Testament, the Word manifests its Face: the invisible Image of the Father, announced and promised through so many centuries, incarnates itself in Jesus of Nazareth, bringing forth the new fundamental attitude of the vision: **"Blessed are the eyes which see the things you see!"** (Lk 10:23).

Saint Irenaeus (second century) said: "When the Word of God was made flesh, He made the image appear in all its truth by becoming Himself that image and He reestablished resemblance by making man entirely similar to the invisible Father." From its origins and now for two millenia, the Christian Tradition presents this decisive faith: God manifests Himself to human beings through the image and the image is the very place of their encounter.

Given that Christ is the consubstantial Image with the

Father (consubstantial meaning that Christ is of the same substance as the Father, that He is God as well), the entire movement of creation and of revelation goes from the Word to the Image. Without its realization in the Image, the Word is incomplete and does not know fulfillment; words alone can lead us to a vague and doubtful imaginary realm or to a sterile abstraction. God is a theory if He remains in His heaven. If God had not manifested His Image among us in Jesus Christ, then we would not have a path toward resembling Him. We are wanderers and remain on our earth. According to the great leitmotif of the Fathers: "God becomes man so that man might become god;" God wants, through His great love, to experience man so that man, through that same love, might experience God; God imprints in the face of human beings His own Image so that, through it, we can begin to resemble Him. Love is always a matter of osmosis, of copenetration, of reciprocity. Without the Image-Prototype, we ultimately have no "mold" (the expression of Saint Augustine) and cease to be ourselves. That absence is where the decomposition of Christianity finds its origin. That which comes out of this concept of humanity—art, culture, civilization—also falls into decadence with absence of His image. Nothing has either source or structure and "ground zero" where the doors of hell open wide is not far off.

THE ICON AS THERAPY

Most of the time, an icon makes us first "react" and we find it "beautiful" or we reject it. This is the level of psychic reaction, the seeking of emotion through aesthetic beauty, the judgement which keeps it at a distance. In his *Three Studies on the Icon*, Eugene Troubetzkoy states that "as long as we are seduced by the pleasures of the flesh, the icon will not speak to us. When it does speak to us, it will be to announce the highest joy, the supra-biological meaning of life and the end of the kingdom of the 'Beast'."

At a first approach, the icon can manifest itself as a powerful revealer of our identity. It may tell us who we are through a simple gaze upon our reactions. As in a mirror, it may unveil us in our attitude and let us know the stage of the journey of our soul (psyche) toward our spirit (being), and becomes an admirable instrument of discernment. The icon can be a therapy.

If our gaze remains upon her, we can go through a "fast of the eyes" (Saint Dorothy, fourth century). This is the time of necessary purification, during which all the senses may reorient and find their true direction. As with the Gospel, the icon usually is a great shock to the one who first enters it. The experience shakes up our system of thought and our order of functioning: "I will destroy the wisdom of the wise, and bring to nothing the cleverness of the clever" (1 Co 1:19). We have no depth, axis or center when our reference point is reason and feeling. When tyrannized by our intellect and emotions, we live only in the spirit of the world with its own categories. Our eyes are imbued with images of the "world," their vision is falsified through the conditioning which we impose upon them: television, newspapers, films, and the walls of our cities of materialism. We undergo a true brainwashing and ultimately put on the glasses of those who manipulate us and live mired in the shortsighted view of appearances, in a restricted life.

The icon makes us penetrate into an entirely different universe. It purifies our gaze and tears down the walls which surround us and which make us believe that this world is our only reality. This purification is a lengthy work, but the more our eyes bathe in the light of icons, the more they desire to do so as the scales fall away. This perpetual irradiation of the icons is a reflection of the uncreated Light of God, an "ecstasy of light" for the eyes come out of their darkness. They begin to see other things in new ways. It is a gaze which is now illumined and apprehends the transparence of all things.

Our whole being enters into the light: **"The lamp of the body is the eye,"** said Jesus. **"If therefore your eye is good, your whole body will be full of light; but if your eye is bad, your whole body will be full of darkness."** (Mat 6:22-23) Contrary to the word and to writing which can go on at length by utilizing reason, the icon is a place of synthesis where multiplicity and opposites are seized in one glance. This unity of the icon and of the eye opens the heart which is also one. And through the heart which is our center, Beauty illumines our whole being. It is through the icon that theology becomes truly experiential.

We neither know our being nor the world, but only their images. Yet the latter does not attain its truth except through the fullness of the mystery represented by the icon.

At its contact, the image which we have created of ourselves and of the world (and sometimes of God Himself) is completely modified. The icon goes through the layers of the conscious and unconscious and enlightens and transforms the multitude of images which swarm in our depth. Psychology has taught us, since C. G. Jung, that it is these images of our subconscious which color our vision of things and beings. They dictate our behavior, and especially our "inexplicable" reactions. They are the obstacle par excellence to all true encounter since they falsify all our relationships: with ourselves, with others and with God. These images always insert themselves between us and the reality that we encounter: we do not see reality as it is, but only through these deceitful filters. From this situation come our judgements and reactions, our mutual misunderstandings, our behavior often so bizarre, along with all the strange things of which people are capable!

The icon plunges its light into this darkness and little by little transfigures our subconscious **"That whoever believes in Me should not abide in darkness."** (Jn 12:46). This is the very process of sanctification. Saint Maximus the Confessor (seventh century) said: "A saint is someone who no longer has a subconscious." Everything in him has become light. Since beauty has direct access to the heart, the person who contemplates an icon enters into the immediate perception of God. Images and thoughts are then filled, pierced by the vivid and burning sensation of the unique Image which creates us from the beginning and endlessly heals us.

"The visualized image has a profound action on the one who practices it," said Dr. Lefebure in *Rhythmic Breathing*. Once again, science merely confirms the old experiences of our Tradition. This action is well known in the contemplation of icons and that is why Christ Himself has taught by means of images and parables.

SEEING, CONTEMPLATING, AND TOUCHING THE UNTOUCHABLE

The veneration of icons is a logical consequence of one's faith in the reality of the Incarnation of Christ. The old platonic dualism, separating flesh from spirit, is definitively overcome. The Word which becomes flesh reveals that not only is matter capable of carrying spirit, but there is also a total and indivisible copenetration. In essence, matter is a condensation of spirit, the very place where life takes shape. The body is the visible expression of that which is invisible, the physical manifestation of that which is metaphysical, the location where we can see, contemplate, touch the Untouchable (1 Jn 1:1). The body carries the Beyond skin deep! This is what the Gospel tells us on every page: "He is the image of the invisible God" (Col 1:15).

In contact with this vision of the divine Beauty, our desire for the divine Love is set ablaze in our hearts and we are as of now secretly illumined and penetrated by the light of the Holy Spirit. Thanks to the perception of the holiness which is transparent in the visible form, we are also sanctified by the powerful energy of the Spirit.

This is not idolatry or magic, but liturgy to which the icon is intimately linked. Whether the icon is in the church or in the home, it accompanies the liturgy and prolongs it throughout daily life: the liturgy immerses us in the right vision, forges a manner of seeing and exercises us in the communication with the Beyond through a slow transformation of oneself. It is in this transformation that the icon participates and which it also carries in itself. It often happens while contemplating an icon that the inner ear will open and hear in one's depths the words heard in the liturgy which celebrate the mystery of this icon. An ineffable atmosphere surrounds the icon and allows the gaze to open onto a reality never seen before. This is the experience of the disciples at Emmaus: they walk with the resurrected Christ and do not recognize Him! It is only after having heard the Word of God and celebrated the Eucharist that "their eyes were opened, and they knew Him" (Lk 24:31). And yet, at the very first gaze upon an icon, while the eyes are still blind, it exercises a strange fascination which calls forth the desire to go further: "Abide with us" say the disciples at Emmaus (Lk 24:29).

The icon is therefore sacramental: it has no reality as does the Eucharist whose bread and wine are truly the Body and Blood of Christ; the icon is only a piece of wood, but it participates in holiness through resemblance and manifests a presence, a "theophany" (as stated by the seventh council in 787). In any case, there can be confusion on this level: the word "icon" clearly states that it is an image and not reality; but the resemblance of the image with its prototype engages us in a real communion with the person represented. The relationship with the icon is mystical in essence. The invisible world is always truly present, much more objective than all that is visible. The icon allows the invisible to radiate visibly; the "supernatural" does not actually exist for divine life is not above nature, but intimately "mixed" with it (Gregory of Nyssea, fourth century). The saints' approach to the Beyond is therefore quite natural, entirely realistic, and thanks to the icon they become part of our daily life: we treat them like every other living person in our entourage; we look at them, we speak to them, we touch them and hug them, for their presence is a word and their silence creates an atmosphere of prodigious radiance.

THE ICON SINGS OF ANOTHER POSSIBLE LIFE

It is not the nature of the divine essence that the icon manifests for it remains forever inaccessible. The icon sends us back to the prototype, makes us grasp the presence of the Person and of the divine energies. It is not a portrait that we face when we are before an icon of Christ or of some saint, but a transparence to their true presence.

The absence of perspective, the disproportion of the represented persons, their form dematerialized by stylization provoke a shock to our visual habits which always seek to objectify and define. Our own perspectives are turned upside down. Our gaze is invited to rest, to become open and receptive, for it is we who are being looked at. The reduction of the icon to two dimensions produces an inverted perspective: the lines go toward the exterior so that the center of the icon is found in the one who looks at it and awakens in the heart of this person the mystery which it represents. At the very center of time and space, the icon opens onto an abyss of transcendence and suggests a path toward the Beyond. Everything is oriented toward this point of extreme openness: there is no heavy and opaque objectification, everything is light, celestial, literally transfigured: the divine figure shows through the material world. Even the clothing is transparent. The bodies have nothing earthly, they are no longer of this world though they yet remain present here. They live in another universe.

The apparent physical immobility of the represented persons translates an extraordinary power of spiritual movement. For them, "all flesh is silent," as is sung in the liturgy, and as all true dance culminates in immobility because its joy has become internal, so the icons show forth the higher intensity of a being who has reached his goal. This astonishing copenetration of unshakable stability and incandescent movement finds its ultimate concentration in the eyes. The eyes are always painted last by the iconographer. After that, there is nothing more to say. This is the point of final convergence where everything is fire through the supreme vision. And that is also our place of encounter with the saints, when our gaze is burned by theirs.

In its very structure, in immobility and movement, in its rhythm, contours, and composition, in the variety of its colors, the icon is poem, a song of adoration and praise. It sings and dances of another possible life. Every color is a radiance which touches us on another level of depth and consciousness. This is knowledge through vibration. We enter through resonance and are brought into harmony with it. There is not a single color which does not have a specific meaning, both in the unveiling of the divine mystery and in its contact with the body of the one who looks on.

ICONOGRAPHY AS MINISTRY

We can see that the technique of the icon is entirely absorbed by its content in the sense that, once mastered, it becomes itself path, transparence, and prayer. The unconditional submission and obedience of iconography to traditional canons expresses the spiritual attitude at its ascetic and mystical heights.

It is this emptiness of self which makes it possible for God to act fully and to enter into synergy with the painter. The icon is then the fruit of a creative act that is always unique. There are never two identical icons even though they are rigorously done according to the same canons. Through ascetiscism and prayer, the painter enters into a certain contemplative vision; the incessant work on himself makes him more and more transparent to the action of the Holy Spirit who is the true iconographer.

The indispensable soil for this synergy is the Church. That is where the painter finds both his nourishing earth, the place where he receives himself, and the elements of his own spiritual growth. That is where his work "situates" itself in the deepest meaning of the word: an icon exists only through its environment which is the Church, the great Tradition, the liturgy and the sacraments, just as a text of Holy Scripture exists only through its context. The icon is born and grows in this soil just like a tree; that is also where it is constantly watered by prayer and where it offers its fruits to the Communion of Saints. Finally, it is there and there alone that the icon is verified in its authenticity according to the criteria of the Fathers.

The requirements of iconography are very high for its responsibility is enormous. Its "job" is a ministry. The Tradition has always assimilated the iconographer with the priest. His piece of wood is an altar where he doesn't paint in reality but prays and celebrates the Holy Mysteries, in the Church and for the Church. His personal path and his mission find their substance in each other. The more he himself advances on the path of holiness, the more he is in communion with the prototype whose resemblance he wants to express through painting. Everything depends on this spiritual experience of the painter that alone is the source of a transmission of beauty and vivifying power. The icons penetrate and install themselves in human hearts, inducing a manner of living and of understanding the world. This is their role, and the role of the iconographer is to work on himself: his transparence allows the transparence of his works and offers the Holy Spirit the freedom to inspire him, to create new forms from the ancient ones which "eye has not seen" (1 Cor 2:9). As long as he has not reached that point, the iconographer will always be asked to rigorously stick to the rules established by the saints that have come before him.

But even an icon perfectly realized according to the canons will never be perfect in relation to its prototype! The important thing is that it show us the way toward the latter, without too many detours or obstacles. The rest is the work of the Spirit in the one who prays before this icon. There have been "ugly" icons down through history that were nevertheless so charged with prayer and love by all those who approached them that they became miraculous and attracted great crowds. The transparence of the one who looks on opens him to his inner icon whose beauty infinitely surpasses the one before his eyes that is only its dim reflection. But the individual miracle is not the criterion of iconography nor the norm of the Church. It belongs to the latter to maintain the universal norm that is a miracle for all: the coming of God among human beings, the Incarnation. There alone is found plenitude.

THE ICON: REVELATION OF BEAUTY

Since God has revealed His face in Jesus Christ, He offers Himself to our contemplation: **"He who has seen Me has seen the Father"** (Jn 14:9) and **"Blessed are the eyes which see the things you see"** (Lk 10:23). Only Beauty makes us truly happy and without her life is not possible; as Dostoevsky wrote, it is Beauty that saves the world. But this is an absolute Beauty that no longer limits the gaze and makes everything transparent, immersing the least thing in the abyss of its mystery, for the invisible now reveals itself as visible. This Beauty is therefore the Word, the one that seizes the eye of the heart to which it has direct access. This experience is always a shock, an awakening, the beginning of change. Such a Beauty never fails us: its direct contact with the human heart is due to the fact that it dwells there and that we are its temples. The durable joy that it opens us to is that of the Kingdom of Heaven in our depths. It cannot be confused with the ephemeral pleasure of an aestheticism in which so many artists project their subjective and emotional world.

Through the revelation of Beauty, the icon leads us over the threshold of the sensible and the psychological, opening the doors of the temple and placing us face to face with the Transcendent. We are not before the work of an author but before the Author of all works. And this does not occur objectively, at a distance, seeing Him three yards away, but in the burning relationship with a personal God.

This explains why there is in Orthodox churches such a sensation of life and of presence. Everything is celebration, even outside of the liturgy, and everything brings us back to the only truly living reality, to the **"one thing needed"** (Lk 10:42): the divine mystery. And when we bow in front of the icons before embracing them, there is someone within who knows that nothing is more intimate to us.

THE ICON TRANSFORMS THE ATMOSPHERE OF THE HOME

These same icons also find their place in the home and

make a temple of it; they sanctify it and their radiance transforms the atmosphere, neutralizing negative vibrations. They give to the dwelling and to all who live there a center where nothing of this world has the last word; everything opens itself toward a Beyond of light and joy. "May your home be a church," said Saint John Chrysostom (fourth century). There, under the icon's gaze of fire and gentleness, love becomes the alchemy of another world. The family cell introduces in its smallest detail the "die and become" of the Easter that never ceases to be celebrated in the liturgy. Life then circulates from one place to another to do its work of transfiguration. Like a candle lit at the side of the icon, we awaken to watchfulness through these constant reminders. Exposed to the icon, we begin to reflect on "the glory of God in the face of Jesus Christ" and we are little by little transformed into this same icon, "beholding as in a mirror the glory of the Lord, are being transformed into the same image" (II Co 3:18; 4:6).

The most extraordinary icon of God, then, is the human being. We become that which we contemplate. And that is why, during the celebration at the church, the priest sends incense upon the faithful as well as upon the icons!

That is also why a relationship between two human beings is never banal and utilitarian: it is the place of a mysterious Visitation where something can begin to dance in the depths of the heart. Judgment or critical gaze upon the other fall back upon their author to accuse him of a frightening nearsightedness. Such a person has a darkened eye and sees only appearances.

The one who is familiar with icons bathes in their light. Indeed, it is light that qualifies an icon. As the Tradition says: an iconographer paints with light and not with colors. According to the days of creation described in Genesis, he moves from the darkness, first placing the darkest layers on the wood, then moves toward a "progressive clarification," from layer to layer until the explosion of light. It is with this Light, which is Christ, that God creates the world, and it is with this same Light that the iconographer works. The uncreated Light emanates from the depths and illuminates the faces. As the center of the icon is located in the person looking at it, it immerses him in this "The true Light which gives light to every man" (Jn 1:9). There it rejoins the light that already inhabits him and opens the path toward illumination.

In this sense, every person can be an iconographer. If there is light in his gaze toward the other, he covers him with splendor and calls forth that which is best in him; the divine spark begins to radiate in his being and the darkness vanishes. Who does not have memories of such an encounter? Only this visionary gaze, learned over a long time by the light of the icons, knows how to contemplate the true beauty of beings and of things. "The eye of the dove" captures and understands the transparence of all that surrounds it. There are no more relationships of power, only Power in relationships. The face is seen as an abyss of mystery: love alone enters into the sanctuary.

THE ICON AS CROSSROAD OF ETERNITY AND TIME: THE PRESENT MOMENT

An icon rests in gold which is light-energy rising from the inaccessible God. He who approaches and enters into this radiance of divine glory with fear and adoration "participates in this energy and becomes light himself" (Saint Gregory Palamas, fourteenth century). When, thanks to prayer and asceticism, this person is completely illuminated by the light, then "he is united with God both spiritually and corporally" (Saint Symeon the New Theologian, eleventh century). His whole being radiates and he becomes the carrier of this light while he lives in the world. This is what Christ calls us to: **"I am the light of the world—you are the light of the world"** (Jn 9:5, Mt 5:14). We receive it from Him through contemplation and become its living flames. Saint Seraphim of Sarov (nineteenth century) was described by his contemporaries as a sun who could hardly be looked upon at certain times. All people will some day be like him, and there are undoubtedly no limits to this growth in the light that is God in person.

Because its perspectives are inverted and due to its liturgical context, the icon descends into the heart of the one who gazes upon it. It is always the movement of Incarnation: as God has descended toward humanity and never ceases to descend right into our darkness and our hell, so the icon descends and gives of itself. The icon invades darkness with its light (Jn 1:5), it fills terrestrial space with heaven. It opens the opaque event of the present to the mystery of eternity which it comes to unite with, and introduces the Beyond at the center of time. The icon is the point where eternity and time meet, it is the center of a cross, that moment which we do not know how to name and which we call for lack of anything better "the present moment;" Plato called it the "sudden, this reality of strange sort"; the Fathers such as Saint Basil called it "the place of encounter of the uncreated and the created and of that which is passed from one to the other," and Saint Gregory of Nyssea (fourth century): "the original influx, the beginning principle, the perpetual birth." We could not describe an icon any better. The fall has corrupted time, it has become "lost time" or "dead time," the "great devourer of peoples"; the radiance of the icon restores it to its heavenly splendor when it was a time of celebration, a time of wedding and friendship between humans and God, the time of the Covenant.

The one who seeks to live in the present moment, in a permanent watchfulness, knows that this is an almost heroic challenge for our human abilities. We are endlessly in the past or in the future and therefore we do not live, since living is here and now, in this precise moment. We have no other treasure than this one! The icon, with liturgy and prayer, is certainly the grand location of this apprenticeship. There, before the icon, everything becomes simple as long as we are receptive. Eyes fixed on the beauty of the Beloved, wonder invades us and its Beauty transfigures time, metamorphosizing us. Instead of a dead time forever repeating itself, a time of absence and void which sometimes makes us dizzy before its non-being, the icon fills time with Presence and Light; with it, each moment becomes an absolute beginning, it is always "as though it were the first time," the wall between time and eternity crumbles. The moment of supreme emptiness, in the face to face encounter, can become supreme plenitude. Fallen time is transformed into deified time. And although the icon is composed of the cosmic scale—the mineral world is present in the colors, the vegetable in the wood, the animal through glue and egg, the human through the saints—it focalizes the whole of creation "which groans and labors with birthpangs" (Rom 8:22) toward this point of divinization.

THE ICON AS LIVING FORGE OF HUMANITY FROM ITS CONCEPTION

What is most extraordinary is that the icon, along with the

liturgical chant, forges human beings from our conception. The mother who contemplates icons and lives with them feeds the little one she carries. He is impregnated in depth, just as the whole liturgy impregnates him: the spiritual life then blossoms and grows in him along with his body and his soul; he no longer comes into the world handicapped in his spirit. The newborn suckles all day and night to nourish his body; he is in a state of total receptivity to awaken and develop his soul: seeing, hearing, touching, speaking; but if his gestation is lived in a spiritual environment, the baby will also be fascinated by the icons as though he had always seen them and he will be spontaneously "at home" in the liturgy! "The image acts profoundly on the human soul, on its creative or motor faculties," Saint John of Kronstadt specifies (1829-1909): "We say, for example, that if during the time which precedes the birth of a child, a mother frequently looks upon the face or portrait of her beloved husband, the child will greatly resemble its father; or if she frequently looks upon the portrait of a beautiful child, she will give birth to a pretty baby."

If then a Christian often looks with love and piety upon the image of our Lord Jesus Christ, of His very pure

Mother and of the saints, His soul will receive the spiritual traits of the lovingly contemplated face: gentleness, humility, mercy, temperance. If we contemplate more often the images and especially the life of the Lord and of His saints, how we will change, how we will travel from height to height! What is as old as the millenia of our Orthodox tradition is today confirmed by scientific research. An orchestra conductor, for instance, knew by heart a piece of music which he had never seen: questioning his mother on this curious phenomenon, he learned that she had studied the piece in question during her pregnancy. But this "by heart" phenomenon is not merely a matter of a curiosity or "secrets" still unknown to human nature. It is also a knowledge that can only come through the heart.

Through the icon and the liturgy, the heart, that is to say the deep center of our being, is opened. This is a bridge toward the other bank, toward the Beyond within. For this child, everything and not only the icon is a window open onto the invisible; everything sings and dances before the beauty of God everywhere present. And of course, "the very face of its father who leans into the crib is the first of all the icons that it contemplates from birth," as Virgil

Georghiu so admirably puts in *The Twenty-fifth Hour*.

Over the years, an illumination of consciousness will occur within the child. The specialists say that at the age of four years, the child has been fully "imprinted," the nerve centers are in place and everything that occurred to that point is of critical importance. Even before the child pronounces his first word, the icon acquaints him, not through theory which is of little use to him but through experience or symbiosis, with all the great mysteries revealed by the Church. With the feasts of the liturgical year represented by the icons, with the saints who show the child his destiny from the beginning of his life, the ultimate meaning of his existence, the only possible way to happiness offered by God to human beings.

Saint Macrina (fourth century) relates in a dialogue with her brother, Saint Gregory of Nyssea, that she said the name of Jesus before knowing how to say "Mama." As the mother's flesh has become the child's flesh on the physical level, so on the spiritual level the child is in-formed by Christ and the form of Christ is within him. This is the very goal of the icon. It makes present and alive the persons whom it represents and the child feels itself part of their universe. The invisible world is as real and palpable as the visible one. He is never far from the icon, always wants to touch it and it is sometimes difficult to take him away from it. This is because the icon is part of his own substance and contemplation is innate to his nature.

Later on, when the child heads off toward his autonomous life, when he marries, when he leaves on trips or simply when he must assume a responsibility, the parents bless him with an icon that they offer to him for his new Path. And the icon accompanies him in all the wanderings of his life. This is an old tradition of the Orthodox countries, still very much alive in our day in Russia and Greece. And when the adult, weighed down by age, will have finished receiving himself from the icon and giving himself to it, it will be given to him again in his casket. It will have done many miracles throughout his life, diffused so much splendor in the darkness, and enlightened many problems; perhaps it will have even saved him from danger and death or healed him from illness, as was so often the case throughout history; now it opens wide the doors of life to this man on whom the casket is closing: **"Enter into the joy of your Lord."** (Mt 25:21) Now the definitive icon presides at our eternal wedding.

OUR FACES RADIATE WITH THE GLORY OF GOD

Before the icon, the prayer of Moses, "Show me Your glory" (Ex 33:18) and that of the Psalms, "Do not hide Your face from me" (Ps 27:9), a prayer which is in the depths of every person, finally finds the path of an answer. We intuit that the *shekinah*, the Glory of God rests on us, as it rested on the Ark of the Covenant. "Do you not know that your body is the temple of the Holy Spirit"? (1 Co 6:19). And we also know that our own face is inhabited by the Holy Face. The tragedy of human freedom is our tendency to close off our face in anguish, death, decay, and even to make it take on the "mask of the beast" (saint Gregory of Nazianzius, fourth century).

Before the icon, the glory of God envelops us as did the cloud that descended on the Temple of Solomon in the Old Testament, and the face of Christ illuminated by a love stronger than death shines upon us. This is not a metaphor or pious words, but the very reason for our creation and that which is effectively realized as soon as we enter the

107

way! Revelation is very clear on this subject: we are created in the image (icon) of God and made to resemble Him. "But we all, with unveiled face beholding as in a mirror the glory of the Lord, are being transformed into the same image from glory to glory" (2 Co 3:18).

When someone finds himself before an icon, or before a word of the Bible, the Holy Spirit immediately moves in his depths to accomplish this work which is truly His own. "The Spirit with His radiance which illumines the Son penetrates our consciousness and fortifies in it the capacity to know the Son, and through Him, the Father" (Dumitru Staniloae, *Prayer of Jesus and Experience of the Holy Spirit*). He introduces the divine energy in our depths which disperses itself in us through the vision of the icon and makes us participate in the life of the Divine Trinity itself. That is the only goal of an icon, whatever its content: to make us enter into the intimacy of God. According to Father Staniloae: "Our consciousness only feels at ease in another consciousness, in the embrace of the loving consciousness of another Person." Before the face of Christ, we recognize the truth of our own faces; we let ourselves be penetrated by His radiance and feel His light on our skin which renders us transparent to our eternity within. To contemplate Him associates us to His immensity, for He takes us into His peace. We are in Him and He is in us; the icon operates this grafting where eternal life begins as of now. As Jesus said: **"And this is eternal life, that they may know You, the only true God, and Jesus Christ whom You have sent"** (Jn 17:3). The word "know," in the Biblical sense, admirably expresses the content of our relationship with the icon: to be born with Him, in Him. Our finitude is engulfed in the limitless Love that looks at us. And in this infinite communion, we decipher our mystery, we are named; the secret of our being is unveiled in the brilliance of the Sun of righteousness. In our night, we see the Invisible.

This is a reciprocal divine-human transparence in which God extends His light into infinity and we advance in this endless becoming. The illumination of human consciousness by God is the path of our divinization. The two, God and the individual, are born together: in their union God becomes human and we become god.

We are born to that which is unique within us—the Person, that unfathomable mystery whose light is carried by our consciousness. We can see here how fragile words are and the limitations of a theology without icons. Through the icon, the words stated by theology are immediately offered to experience; the Word effectively becomes flesh, the heart becomes intelligent and the intelligence becomes cordial, words catch fire, thought is warmed and experience knows the amplitude of its meaning. We exist within the action of the Word and of the Spirit that open the divine entrails and our depths at the same time. The light of my consciousness is Presence; it may only be a feeble glow for the moment, but by immersing its gaze into the icon, it can deploy itself toward infinite and always new spaces.

CONTEMPLATING AS CHERUBIM

Yet, just as to perceive a word in depth takes careful listening, so too must we remain a good while in contemplation in order to learn the language of the icon. In general, we judge and pass on, but here we must stop and remain, then let ourselves go for a long time. The action of the icon is deep and lengthy during the whole of the liturgy which is its privileged place. But this liturgical action is also pursued in the prolonged face to face encounter at home. We can sit before the icon or remain standing. Those who are in the habit of meditating can take a posture, sitting on their heels or on a little bench. But whether sitting or standing, it is always important to relax at the beginning, especially in the neck and shoulders, and to breath deeply from the abdomen.

The aim is to become a receptive cup, to be fully conscious, and no longer objectify or maintain external things at a distance. Every physical tension accompanied by upper chest breathing is a closure, leading to suspicion and inevitably to a power struggle with the external. Judgement is then inserted between the self and the object: the experience of encounter is impossible; we see without seeing. Jesus tells us: **"And seeing you will see but not perceive"** (Mt 13:14). The object is in our head, intellectualized, and it does not descend into the heart. There is knowledge but no understanding, and therefore no transformation.

Profound relaxation is complete openness and makes possible a completely different way of seeing things. Our gaze no longer judges or fixes things, but receives and contemplates. It not only makes use of the eyes but also of the nape of the neck and the spinal cord, and finally of the whole body which now sees like the cherubim (the angels) "with multiple eyes." The liturgy will have taught us this way which consists in discovering the depths of sensorial qualities: simply to see, without any thought or interpretation whatsoever. To see, to bathe in the sensation of the sight, to let the colors penetrate within, along with the lines and the forms and the mystery, without commentary. Feel the act and don't think it.

As we have already stated, we are today verifying scientifically that which the Tradition knows through revelation and experience: a sensation received in a pure state (without interpretation) operates a disconnection of the nerve centers and invades the whole field of consciousness. It establishes a kind of silence of the brain, for we cannot think and feel at the same time. That is a great secret which opens the way to mystical experience and which is the very foundation of the hesychast tradition (*hesychia* means silence). Dr. Vittoz (died 1925) was one of the first to initiate what he called a "Method of cerebral control" where through simple feeling, he healed many neuroses and even cases of mental paralysis. He observed that "sensation is not only an experience of extraordinary relaxation, but of unification of the whole person, a recreation of self, a journey toward liberation." But he especially pointed out, and this is what interests us most, that the more we enter into sensation, into the interiority of feeling, **"abide in Me, and I in you"** (Jn 15:4), the more we discover that which the Fathers called "the sensation of the Divine." The moment of sensation is necessarily that of presence, presence to self, presence to God. The mystery that we contemplate on the icon is our own reality. A sensation (not an emotion) of peace, of joy and love can then literally inundate our being. These are the "fruit of the Spirit" of which Saint Paul speaks (Ga 5:22) and the criteria verifying the authenticity of our experience.

WONDER: THE KEY TO ALL KNOWLEDGE

These "fruits" of the spirit are also "instruments" to go unceasingly further on the spiritual journey. Wonder has always been considered, beginning with the ancient Greek philosophers, as one of the greatest means of knowledge. The icon is both the means and the path of realization. In this sense, according to Goethe, "wonder is the summit of what human beings can become." Through wonder, we feel ourselves placed at the origin of all things, as though we were participating in the creative act and in the wonder of God Himself before His creature. This is an experience of the "breakthrough of Being" (as Karlfried Graf Dürckheim called it), where we are completely seized and, because we have found our origin beyond our nature, we find that distress linked to this fallen nature disappears: the fear of death, the meaninglessness of life and solitude.

The person who cultivates wonder discovers this original freedom and goes through life like a troubadour. The immense joy with which Life gratifies him causes him to dance with inexplicable happiness. The most extraordinary example that best personifies all this (obviously after Mary), is Saint Francis of Assisi. We have often remembered only the stigmatas identifying him with the suffering Christ, forgetting that he identified himself much more to the resurrected Christ who caused "perfect joy" to be born within him. The two mysteries, the death and resurrection of Christ, which are inseparable, generated in Francis such wonder that he saw their presence everywhere. He contemplated the glory of God not only on the icons of his time (which were the last vestiges of the icon in the West of the thirteenth century; some can still be seen in the Saint Clare basilica at Assisi), but since the icon teaches us this gaze, he could see glory in the least blade of grass, as is witnessed to in his admirable *Canticle of the Creatures*. The Franciscan monk Eloi Leclerc tells us in his book *The Wisdom of a Poor Man* that Francis said to brother Leon: "To discover that God is God, eternally God, beyond what we are or can be, to fully rejoice in what He is, to find ecstacy before His eternal youth and give thanks because of who He is, because of His perfect mercy, such is the deepest requirement of this love which the Spirit of the Lord forever pours out into our hearts. That is what it means to have a pure heart."

We know of no more beautiful description of the fruit of the icon in the human heart. This is the very fruit of holiness, and this formidable wonder, this spirit of childhood rediscovered, is necessarily part of every saint. The being who is in wonder sees the essential beyond appearances, and contemplates the mystery which is inaccessible to analysis or to habitual mental categories. We are seized: this is the true mode of a global consciousness.

That is why philosophers have always sought it out. Heidegger, one of the most eminent of our contemporaries, stated: "It is much more important to let oneself be seized than to understand!" This is the vocabulary of the Gospels: "Let yourself be taken," said Saint Paul.

TERROR AND FASCINATION

Quite often, deep immersion into the icon provokes a seizing of grace in the one who contemplates it: an inexplicable joy inundates his heart and plunges him into prayer beyond all words. The biography of the iconographic saints Andrew Rublev and Daniel Cernjy relate that at feast days when they did not paint, sitting in silence before the icons, "the radiance of a holy joy filled them." In the same way, Saint John Damascene (eighth century) said that the icons "captivate my sight and lead my soul into the praise of God."

It is important to understand this phenomenon—the passage from the psychological level to the ontological level, from the soul to the spirit. It is in this passage that is found the meaning of the "spiritual" path. Our spirit is completely seized by the divine light. Its mode of knowing is not like the intelligence of the soul which operates through deduction, reflection, analysis, synthesis; the spirit knows through grasping before anything is even formulated; this is the inner contemplative look of wonder.

The spirit sees and operates through vision, and that is why one of its characteristics is light: it is illumined when it sees. And as it lives only through God, it is attracted above all by the splendor of God and the splendor of glorified creation which is its reflection. It is fascinated by beauty. True beauty always gives direct access to the heart-spirit. That is why the criterion of the authenticity of beauty is joy which is the fruit of the spirit, a durable and indelible joy which only the spirit can give.

Beauty is the face of God. Psalm 45 says of Christ: "You are fairer than the sons of men." But Saint Paul reminds us that Christ is the "effigy of the Father," and the Holy Spirit is His brilliance. If our spirit is so sensitive to splendor, it is because splendor dwells within it, is its substance and our spirit recognizes it all around. It can be seized by it through everything and as the spirit opens, this gaze becomes constant and no longer loses sight of Being spread out in all things. All teaching on the icon seeks to awaken us to this gaze. This seizing opens onto adoration, which is the inevitable attitude of the one who experiences the sacred. The seized person internally prostrates himself, and always feels that which Rudolf Otto calls "terror and fascination" (in *The Idea of the Holy*), the fear before the Wholly Other, the extreme transcendence of God which has nothing in common with human beings. Saint Peter cries out, "Distance yourself from me, Lord, I am only a sinner," and yet there is also a sensation of fascination here, for we know that we are ultimately promised light and joy, for life itself is nothing but that.

We can then prostrate ourselves: either at length, forehead to the ground before the icon, in the posture of Elisha or prostrate oneself and rise as many times as desired. Certain monks prostrate themselves hundreds of times a day. Before the amazing Presence, we first feel ourselves as dust and nothingness, and all we can do is prostrate ourselves. Humility comes spontaneously and prostrations open the heart to conversion. The emptiness of self is created in oneself and the Presence can finally enter in.

We discover then that this is a Presence which incarnates itself in our own flesh, as is manifested in the icon of the Nativity. This Presence constantly pulls us from the deep waters of daily life, as Saint Peter shows us while sinking in the stormy sea or as seen in the icon of Christ resurrected pulling Adam from hell. Before these extraordinary mysteries that penetrate us and settle into our consciousness, we feel ourselves restored and saved by the great love of God, in spite of our sin. Fascination invades us, our heart rejoices and our prayer becomes praise: we are touched in that moment by the very substance of the icon which is essentially praise, song, glory. There is identification and the icon has truly reached its goal, for in this experience of joy is found the purpose of it all. The icon makes of wonder a state of being and the Gospel is fulfilled.

Admiration before God, the joy of seeing that God is God, and the praise which is its expression, appear throughout the whole Bible as humanity's reason for being. The person who has understood this and has made it the axis of his own life becomes a free being, first freed from himself because praise tears him away from his ego, then free from all things and even from circumstances. He is stripped, his only happiness is God and that which God wants from him in each moment. This is the "pure heart" and true poverty. Even sin is no longer a burden, for he has given everything, including his worries. For such a person, nothing veils the splendor of God before which he never ceases to rejoice! The beauty of the icon makes us shiver with joy, and joy proves that the beauty of God has penetrated into our depths.

Within praise is revealed the face of God. According to Saint Augustine (fifth century), that is why "praise is the beginning and the end of our relationship with God," for it is also the relationship between the three divine persons. If there is joy in God, it is because God is Love. Without Love, there is no joy. And the purpose of Love is to communicate with us **"so that My joy may remain in you, and that your joy may be full"** (Jn 15:11).

The icon is the place of this communication. Through praise, we open ourselves to the icon and we resemble it. According to the Fathers, joy is truly the fruit of our divinization, and we then resemble God. "As the moon is lit by the sun, our faces are illuminated by the same glory which we see shining on the face of Christ. This glory which transfigures us in a permanent way is the glory of God, eternal, divine, communicated to our bodies. This transmutation of the flesh into spirit is evidently not visible but it is as real as though it were visible" (*Christ in the Theology of Saint Paul*).

BREATHING THE ICON: IT BECOMES OUR FLESH AND BLOOD

Just as the sun communicates its light to the moon, so God communicates His light of glory to human beings. It is precisely for this reason that God created us and this communication is the creative act itself. It is so intimate to God and to human beings that it mixes with their reciprocal breath. God created humanity by breathing into it. I am breathed in by God (Gn 2:7; Ps 104:23,30). Therefore, we really live only by entering into this breath which is an exchange of life, a dialogue of love, a thanksgiving. It is thanksgiving and praise that makes us live and without it we die. We must praise just as we must breathe, for that is where our happiness is found. "Let

121

everything that has breath praise the Lord!" (Ps 150:6). Before the icon this becomes the summit of all prayer: in complete immobility, fully relaxed and surrendered, truly conscious, we must let ourselves be inhaled by God while inhaling the icon with gratitude, and in exhaling, let it penetrate within. It becomes my flesh and my blood, breath imbues my whole being physically, into the least of my cells. Nothing is to remain a stranger to God, there is no darkness that cannot receive light, everything within me is called to transfiguration. The simple fact of breathing in this way, naturally and without augmenting the volume of the breath, places us before that which is most original— the great movement of Life within us.

The icon is the Word that the Father breathes into me and I receive it by inhaling. Through the power of the Spirit-Breath, the Word becomes flesh within me in exhalation. The uncreated light of this triple Presence becomes corporal, the body itself is conscious of it. I can lower my eyes, for the icon is within me now, my body is its temple and my heart expresses its living reality through torrents of praise.

In perfect harmony with the icon is the silence of

contemplation, as Psalm 65:2 clearly expresses in the Hebraic version: "For You alone the silence is praise!" Indeed, the Ineffable corresponds to the Infinite which is beyond all words in the depths of our being. Saint Isaac the Syrian (sixth century), the silent one of the deserts, affirms with power: "When we can no longer support the incandescence of this inner fire, vanquished by joy, we are sometimes obliged to shout" (*Spiritual Writings*). The Church has always understood this and that is why she invites us to sing before the icons: to give free rein to this profound jubilation, but also to call it forth. The Divine Offices before the icons should fill our days. Nothing, in fact, can replace singing. It is through song that the vibration of the icon is best communicated; it places us in the tonality of the icon. If we have not learned to sing, we can take a psalm every day and simply sing it on the same note, *recto tono*. "To love God," said Saint Augustine (fifth century), "is to sing His glory, and better yet, to become oneself a song of glory."

CHAPTER V

AT THE SOURCE OF LIFE

Jesus said: **"Lo, I am with you always, even to the end of the age"** (Mt 28:20). Until then He was present in Palestine, at a particular epoch, among his disciples. With the Ascension, Jesus does not retire behind some mountain of stars to preside over an assembly of former Christians as has often been pictured. On the contrary: He enters into a universal presence, present in all epochs of history, in all countries and places of the world, in the heart of every person. His is a silent and invisible Presence. But at the heart of the Church, this presence continues to be visible and to manifest itself historically through the sacraments. Saint Cabasilas (nineteenth century) stated that "the sacraments are a way, the door which Jesus has opened and it is in passing through this way and this door that Christ returns toward humanity."

THE CHURCH: A SOCIO-POLITICAL SYSTEM OR BODY OF CHRIST?

Unfortunately, we have had for centuries in the West a ritualistic conception of the sacraments. They have become marginal acts which are added to life but do not constitute its essence. As a cultural institution, they are a place where, through the mediation of the clergy, we may procure grace. In the worst cases, the sacraments are only a sociological phenomenon: children are baptized through convention or married in church for the sake of custom. Emptied of their substance, it is not surprising that they have been massively rejected!

Perhaps Christians will someday rediscover the great sacramental tradition of the early times. Christ never wanted these centuries of deviation imposed upon us. The Church was not destined to become a socio-political machine, but the Body of Christ. It is the Church itself which is the great sacrament of Christ being present among us that gives itself to us under many guises in every moment. Christ came to "make all things new" (Rev 21:5) and the Church is the matrix of this birth.

It was to be this way from the beginning: in "blessing" creation, God filled everything with His presence (Gn 1:2), everything that exists is a gift of God to humanity and through everything He wants to make Himself known to us and offer us His love. Everything is grace. When we come in contact with beings and with things in our daily life and give thanks, when we bless in turn all that we touch, then our whole life becomes "eucharistic" (which etymologically means "thanksgiving"), and ultimately a communion with God. We are therefore priests of the creation which we constantly receive from the hands of God and which we offer back to Him. This is our true destiny and the meaning of life, no matter what our work may be.

God has created the world for this universal Eucharist where everything, without exception, is sacrament, that is to say, the place of divine manifestation and loving exchange with humanity. We should have no other work than this one: giving thanks to God, this is the Work within our work. In doing this, we transform the life of the world, the life of every moment, into a life in God. But in failing to do this, we cut ourselves off from God, we live as though God did not exist and make of life the absurd hell which we know so well. We have committed this rupture from the beginning, and we begin it again every day. If we do not seek God, the Absolute, in what we live from moment to moment, everything becomes subjective, opaque and without transparence; things are then encapsulated in themselves, nothing has meaning and we find ourselves permanently unsatisfied. We materialize the world and close it in on itself, instead of opening it onto the Presence and transforming everything into divine joy.

The ultimate meaning of the sacraments is found there. If Christ has come to pull us out of this rupture and to create a new covenant with us, to restore everything in the original intention of creation, it is surely not through a few ritual acts on the periphery of life! On the contrary, worship with Him has meaning only if it transforms the whole of life: **"The hour is coming when you will neither on this mountain, nor in Jerusalem, worship the Father . . . but in spirit and in truth"** (Jn 4:19-24). This fullness of life is therefore Christ himself, offered in each moment, since "He is in all things." As before the fall of humanity, the whole of life is offered as "sacrament," the place of communion with God. Not in this place or that, on the mountain or in Jerusalem, but here and now, in what and where I am in the midst of living.

TO LIVE IS CHRIST

The Church has no greater role than to awaken us to this life and teach it to us. That is why it is the sacrament of Christ, the presence of Christ at the heart of history. The person who lives in the Church is therefore incorporated into Christ: through a slow alchemy, a true osmosis, we are born into Christ and receive His life. According to the powerful expression of Saint Nicolas Cabasilas, we are subject to a "christification": Christ gives us His own eyes, His own limbs, His blood and breath. This is not some pious metaphor, we are not "as" a member of the body of Christ, but we are "truly that," as Cabasilas insists. Our being is completely "christified," transfigured, modeled in the figure of Christ, and all our senses and psychosomatic faculties are metamorphosized in Christ. "The blood through which we live now is the blood of Christ, and our

129

flesh is the body of Christ. We share life in common" (*Life in Christ*).

This astonishing and hardly conceivable reciprocity is the culmination of all creation, and this is a growth which is never completed. We are born into our true dimension, for we are only human if we become god. God alone has fullness of Life; outside of Him, we cannot know happiness. Our truth is found in resemblance to God.

All this is part of the Gospel. Saint Paul sums up the very essence of faith when he says: "It is no longer I who live, but Christ lives in me" (Ga 2:20). But nothing surpasses the realism of Christ himself, whom the disciples hurry away from when he pronounces the stunning words on "the bread of life": **"I am the bread of life . . . and the bread that I shall give is my flesh, which I shall give for the life of the world . . . He who eats this bread will live forever"** (Jn 6:35-58). This is the Eucharist, the sacrament which is at the center of everything, which constitutes the Church and through this sacrament the Church transforms humanity into the Body of Christ— each person, the whole cosmos, as well as all of history. It is, according to Cabasilas, the ultimate reality and the purpose of life; from the beginning, we were created to this end: "If we have received thought, it is to know Christ; we have desire in order to run toward Him; we have memory to carry Him within us for He is Himself the Archetype of those whom He has created . . . What can be more sacred than our body in which Christ entered into more intimately than nature?"

Being "structured" in all our faculties to contain the infinite explains why we inevitably remain unsatisfied if we feed ourselves only with finite and relative things. Before Christ and without Him, no one could be truly happy, observed Cabasilas, for "the object of our desire could be found nowhere"! All desire is therefore a desire for God, and when desire is purified, it is God Himself within us. To feed ourselves of anything else but God is to wrong our desire, to make it miss its original direction. That is why eating the Christ-God in the Eucharist is to rediscover little by little the ontological axis of all our desires in which we can encounter God in all things and "rejoice in Him alone with complete pleasure." Such a life is once again entirely eucharistic. We can bless everything we see and touch, give thanks, take the Eucharist "in all times and places," rejoicing fully in the fact that God is God, for this is the Life of life. The joy which runs through such a person is the sign that this Life triumphs within him, that he has entered into the joy of his Master (Mt 25:21) and has discovered why he was created. Only this joy is capable of transforming humanity and the world; outside of it, there is no mission and no witness. The Eucharist is the sacrament of this joy, its source and continual deepening.

A GREAT MOVEMENT OF TRANSFORMATION

The path of liturgy, its inner unfolding, follows the same stages as meditation, or rather: it is meditation which follows the same stages as the liturgy. There is nothing surprising in this, for it is the same "Jacob's Ladder" by which God descends and humanity rises. It is the "Tree of Life" planted in the lost paradise of our depths or the "Tree of the Cross" which allows us to pass from this dead life to the true Life. There are always four essential stages:

1. LETTING GO

This is the first part of the liturgy, generally known as the "liturgy of the Word." In the processional, the deacon solemnly carries the Bible, places it on the center of the altar where the celebrants salute it by kissing it. This is the Word which becomes flesh and lives in the midst of the people. It will be heard in the great texts of the Scriptures: they are proclaimed by a reader, but it is really the voice of Christ that comes to us! It is surrounded by songs, which themselves are nothing but the Word lovingly repeated until they are completely assimilated.

The Word of God first "prunes" and strips us (Jn 15:2-3); it acts like a sword which cuts and separates, and is a power which unfailingly initiates the effects aimed at by God: "My word from My mouth shall not return to Me void, but it shall accomplish what I please" (Is 55:11). We must cut ourselves off from the world we come from, from the "spirit" of this world which sticks to our being like glue; we must let go of our way of seeing and thinking, of our criteria and of our projects, of our multiple fears which this spirit imposes upon us and by which it fashions us; we must be rid of its false promises, its trickeries and its lies. In fact, we must let go of our own "I," this ego artificially fattened which is the primary obstacle on the path of our transformation. We are in the world, but **"not of the**

world" (Jn 15:19).

When we come to the liturgy, the Word operates a profound and radical rupture within us: all of a sudden, everything is fundamentally other, in the strongest sense of the word: we are completely uprooted. And yet we experience in the deepest part of ourselves, despite our initial shock which sometimes overshadows it, the following experience: faced with the disintegration of the world, and therefore of our own personhood, through sin and death, there is here in this liturgy that which is uniquely necessary, the only reason for living, that toward which all things secretly grow. Everything else can and must be let go. It is only through this disengagement with the world that the new person, washed in the liturgical light, can live differently in this world of darkness and allow God to save him.

The emptiness of such a letting go makes a cup of the human heart, the manger where the Word will descend as Divine Child, the seed of all spiritual growth. In the inner freedom of the person with a pure heart, the Word becomes power, life and sanctification since it will truly incarnate itself in the flesh and blood of the one who listens to it. The Word and the sacrament of the Eucharist are indivisibly linked. The sacrament accomplishes that which the Word announces. If the Word did not truly become our life, our physical substance, it would only be abstraction and ideology. This is the sacrament which verifies its authenticity through the most carnal experience. All those who participate in the liturgy with regularity will testify that at the end of several years they are no longer the same. They see differently and are aware of different things, for their vision is new.

2. GIVING ONESELF

Having been stripped and become poor, we are happy: **"Blessed are the poor in spirit"** (Mt 5:3). Free of all attachments, we can now give ourselves without any lies. In our growth there is never this second step without the first one.

In the second half of the liturgy, we then see the celebrants going toward the altar known as the "prothesis." There, they take the "gifts," the bread and wine, and carry them in a new solemn procession through the church to the altar in the Holy of Holies.

We do not offer to God bread and wine, but as this food is made to live by, it is actually our life which we give: the bread of our daily life, the wine of our joys and of our suffering. But through this bread made with wheat and this wine from the vine, it is in essence all of creation that we offer to God. Liturgy rediscovers here its first orientation toward God and we find our primordial role of being the celebrant of this oblation. The clergy is not "deleguated" to accomplish the office, for it is the whole assembly which celebrates together. At the heart of this liturgy, we undergo an apprenticeship of our life which must become liturgy in its entirety, where each gesture will be a celebration, a movement of love and adoration toward God. The liturgical assembly is truly the "laboratory of a new humanity," the Church.

This new community, which Saint Peter calls "a chosen generation, a royal priesthood, a holy nation" (1 Pt 2:9) can only be born with the birth of persons. A community exists only if each one of its members is born to himself. We only "commune" with others through the best of ourselves, our deep "I," that which we call the person, and not with our masks or our neurotic personalities. The characteristic of the person, this ultimate mystery of our being, is the gift of self. We cannot define personhood, but when we experience it, it always manifests itself as a movement "toward" God or "toward" others. It is an abnegation through which we resemble God who is *Gift* par excellence. Abnegation is the manner in which God acts at the heart of the Divine Trinity: each Person says to the other, "You!" and enters into a total abnegation of Self which makes the other live. But when God manifests Himself to us, it is also through this same abnegation: in love He lowers Himself to the point of dying for us on the cross.

Through this "movement toward," this abnegation or this way of "giving oneself," Jesus reveals to us the key to Life. Death to self is in reality a birth into plenitude. The person who dies voluntarily is born into the divine life, abnegation being the very nature of the human spirit, while pride—life which keeps itself for itself—is anti-abnegation, a dead life. To give oneself is to die voluntarily, and that is the apprenticeship which we undertake in this stage of the liturgy so that we may then live fully at every moment. Behind the most ordinary things of life, there is death and resurrection. This is lived experientially by the "Yes" that our whole being pronounces from moment to moment to all that comes: "Thy will be done!" We do not go beyond duality except through taking up the cross. By accepting the unacceptable with love, this gift of ourselves leads us beyond opposition to Christ and beyond this true manner of giving oneself here and now arises Life. This reality is such an unfathomable mystery that we cannot reach it on our own. Only Christ gave Himself fully, His sacrifice was perfect and He offered us His life. His Life is our life, He is the firstborn in this movement of abnegation and leads us into His own destiny. Also, this procession of saintly gifts symbolizes liturgically the entry of Jesus into Jerusalem to live His death and resurrection there, the supreme gift that sustains us all.

3. SURRENDERING ONESELF

This is the culminating point of letting go. We should not speak of stages or successive parts of the liturgy, but of a single movement where each part contains the whole and continues in the next. This single movement continuously tears us away from the world of darkness and transforms us into participants of the celestial Kingdom. When we release ourselves from ourselves, we enter into in a stage of receptivity and gift. But the measure of the gift, as the Ancients say, is to be without measure, to surrender completely. Like the clay in the hands of the potter (Jr 18:6), our destiny places itself in the hands of Christ, and our two destinies mix, the bread and the wine of our life become His Body and Blood, surrendered in Him.

This is the central part of the liturgy which opens through an immense thanksgiving addressed to the Father of heaven, the Source of all gifts and the Author of the marvels which we celebrate. Only through the astonishing power of thanksgiving and praise do the heavens open and make of the human heart the throne of God. That is what Jesus did: the night of the Last Supper before "giving Himself," He took the bread, "gave thanks" and said: **"Take, eat, this is My body."** Then He did the same with the cup, **"Drink from it, all of you; this is My blood of the new covenant."**

When the priest at the altar repeats these gestures and says these words again, it is not a magical rite or a pious miming, but Reality. Since Pentecost, the Holy Spirit has entered all things, eternity lives in time and time has opened onto the eternal now. When we celebrate the liturgy, we are truly on Golgotha, we truly live the Last Supper, the death and resurrection of Christ, here and now, concretely as witnesses; and when the priest says: **"This is My body . . . ."** we hear the very words of Christ. At that moment, the Holy Spirit is powerfully invoked upon the bread and wine, and His Fire descends on the altar as well. Throughout history, many saints have physically seen it with their eyes, but all have seen it with the eyes of faith and feel it in the shimmering joy surrounding them. And our faith suffices to us, and our joy fills us. The miracle is there in all its realism: there is no more bread and wine, but the flesh and blood of Christ dead and resurrected. The Orthodox Christian does not ask the question of "how," but prostrates himself before the great love of God. His forehead on the dust of the ground, he knows that he would accept to die rather than to renounce this mystery. "It is much more important to let oneself be seized than to understand" (Heidegger). And that is why, once seized in the depths of his being, he must rise and stand to sing out loud: "Christ is resurrected from the dead!" for that is now his own condition.

Indeed, Christ has taken our flesh and blood which we have "surrendered" to Him and, in this identification, we die and are resurrected with Him. There is life only in God, He is the Life and outside of Him, all is death; separated from Him (the state called "sin"), we are dead and live in death, even if appearances seem otherwise. If the Christ-God descends into death, into our death, He vivifies it from within and from death itself surges the definitive Life, resurrection. This is the Easter of Christ and ours as well. Every liturgy is an Easter, and that is why our whole life is paschal. Through His abnegation, His suffering and death, Christ has let enter into Him all the anguish of the fallen world, the hell of the human condition enslaved to hatred and lies, to our suffering and our mortified life; everything has been annihilated by Him and bathed in the light of His resurrection; nothing else can have the last word. "You have descended into the depths of the earth and you have broken the eternal chains which held us captive . . . Through the cross, joy has come into the world" (Easter Hymn composed by Saint John Damascene, seventh century). The tomb is transformed into a nuptial chamber, the resurrected Christ is the groom who comes to us at the heart of every despair. Each difficulty is in fact a sort of death if, after having "let go" of all our resistances, we "surrender ourselves" to it with love. If we accept the difficulty as our own cross through an unconditional "yes" to all that occurs, then all these tombs which are our problems are transformed and we can act in an entirely new and unknown light which has nothing in common with all our negative and destructive reactions. "Now everything is filled with light: the sky, the earth and hell" (Easter Hymn by John Damascene, seventh century).

If each one of us, with all that makes up our life in its smallest details, is dragged into the resurrection of Christ, it is also the case for the whole of humanity which finds itself secretly recreated. We are illumined from within, as is the cosmos and the whole of creation: "Yesterday, I was buried with You, O Christ, today I awaken with You, O Resurrected One . . . By rising from the tomb, You have resurrected with You Adam and his whole race . . . May the whole universe be in celebration for He is resurrected, the Christ, the Eternal Joy" (Easter Hymn).

4. REBIRTH

This is the moment of communion when we receive the Body and Blood of Christ dead and resurrected as well as the Fire of the Holy Spirit. We will therefore be literally assimilated into the wondrous event which we have just lived: we become that which we eat. The messianic banquet to which we are invited incorporates us into Christ resurrected: His Flesh is my flesh, we are co-corporal, and His Blood flows in my veins. This is a real transfusion. "The Spirit breathes Christ into us to the very tips of our fingers" said Saint Symeon (eleventh century). Now, each Eucharist assimilates us a little more into Him, rooting us deeper into the Resurrected One; everything is incandescent with His Presence, our entire life is swallowed up by the resurrection and finds its orientation in it. Next to it, everything is relative, and of all the events of history, the resurrection is the only one which is absolute. "It is the resurrection which gives meaning to history and is its universal gravity," said the patriarch Athenagoras. To the extent that we commune with Christ resurrected, that we live everything in His light, the world and its history begin to be resurrected within us.

For this is the whole point: to let this power of life blossom within us, to resolutely inaugurate in oneself a new way of being; from this inner force of the Resurrected One will come a zeal which will give rise to the solutions of all the social problems of our time. There is no other ferment with which to answer the agonizing and tragic questions of humanity. We often wish to adopt the evangelical values, fighting for justice, peace and love in order to transform the world, but detached from the person of Christ they are not *life giving* and risk becoming embedded in human pride. Did the Christ not say: **"without Me you can do nothing"** (John 15:5)? Intimate communion alone, as between the vine and its branches (Jn 15) will make it possible for the Divine Life to circulate among human beings in a way mere values cannot. Values have never transformed anyone. They may provide a varnish, or sometimes modify the surface, but as long as the center of human beings (the heart) is not reached, nothing great will take place. The transformation of the heart is always a matter of encounter between God and an individual, an experience of fire. An inflamed heart can set fire to the world, and the whole history of the saints is witness to that.

The world belongs to those who are joyful in their hearts, and there is no greater joy than the joy of Easter! It is the very depth of the Gospel and the Eucharist is its sacrament. God created us for this. It is through joy that we best know God and through joy that we are assimilated to Him. There is no better "instrument" for knowing God, for being born within Him, and there is no better "instrument" for conquering the world and transforming it. Joy or thanksgiving takes us out of alienation and returns us to freedom. It is "abundant life" because it is Christ Himself. When offered upon the world, upon each event and upon each moment, thanksgiving allows us to "recognize" their Divine Origin, to see in everything a gift of God and to rediscover the eucharistic attitude when confronted with life. Ultimately, we discover that everything is sacrament and life itself is a liturgy. This is what we experience throughout the day when, leaving the church filled with Divine Life, we return toward the world. Gratitude is the great antidote to pride. From the beginning, pride tears the world away from God to deliver it to all the demons. **"Be of good cheer, I have overcome the world"** (Jn 16:33). Indeed, we do not leave the church when going into the world: those who remain in Christ are the Church, the Body of Christ is present at the heart of humanity "as the leaven is in the bread," in order to transform it completely into Church, the "race of the newly born."

THE TIME OF CELEBRATION

Liturgy is a bath in Divine Glory. Everything else in our spiritual life refers to it and can only be an extension of it. It is truly the testament of Christ, His request: **"Do this in remembrance of Me!"** That is why the Tradition calls Christians "the friends of the celebration." Celebration is in our depths without our knowing it even while we seek it; liturgy reconnects us with these secret yearnings of our being. There, it puts us in touch with the dazzling beauty of Christ resurrected. In this seizing we know the jubilation that stops time which is tragically closed in upon itself like a tomb. The beauty of Christ, with which He seeks to clothe each one of us, is that of the "eighth day"; it is eternal life begun as of now by all those who let themselves be inhabited by Christ.

We all experience some dreariness at the core of our daily life: time is slavery, a fatal and tragic destiny, smelling of nothingness. It is a dismal repetition of the death of each moment, engendering anguish and immersing us into an absurd and diabolical routine. Humanity has only one question: how to free ourselves from this nightmare? "Vanity of vanities . . . one generation passes away, another generation comes . . . the sun also rises, and the sun goes down . . . that which has been is what will be . . . all things are full of labor . . . there is nothing new under the sun . . . " (Ec 1:2-9). This is vertigo before the abyss of lost time.

But in Christ, eternity unites with time and this demonic dizziness gives way to the intoxication of the Spirit. From now on, "we live our whole life as a celebration, certain that God is everywhere, singing in the midst of our work, sailing to the melody of hymns, conducting ourselves in everything as citizens of Heaven. The perfected one constantly links to God the legitimate use of things. His whole life is a sacred liturgy" (Clement of Alexandria, second century). The resurrected Christ has reintroduced the divine plenitude into the heart of time;

147

through His beauty He has returned it to its original splendor. As in the period before the fall, the time of the Church is once again a sacrament: a place of encounter between God and human beings, a time of dialogue and friendship and the wondrous wedding of one to the other. It is the time of miracle, for eternity is constantly near to daily life, and it is a time of celebration because there is no greater wonder! It is also for humanity the "time of vigilance" where, focusing all our energies, it gives to our being both direction and maturity because of our attitude of surrender and love. In other words: it is the time of exercise (the exact translation of the word "asceticism"), where time is a Path on which human freedom is put to the test. Yet it is only time-as-sacrament which allows us to be fulfilled. The sacrament turns everything into grace, in every single moment of our time. By exercising ourselves to live each instant in this grace, it gives us the power to commune with time, to definitively step out of duality. This is the true miracle of the sacrament, for nothing immerses us more into suffering than duality, the nonacceptance of that which is. This is also the true meaning of celebration, for if everything is full of grace, then nothing exists except the joy of "giving thanks in all times and places."

The Ancient Ones, particularly Saint Basil the Great (fourth century), see in all this the very meaning of Sunday: it is both the first and the eighth day, the origin and the end, the moment in which eternity calls forth time and ceaselessly replaces it. It is the first day in which the light of the world was created, the anniversary of creation, and it is the eighth day, that of Easter, the "Day of the Sun that will never set," where the light of the resurrection has flooded the universe. Since Easter is celebrated every day in the Eucharist, these other days of the week, which symbolize the unfolding of the complete becoming of the universe, bathe in the same light and open onto the celestial Kingdom. Each period of the year is also the celebration of mysteries that prepare Easter or fulfill it: the time of Advent and Christmas, the time of Lent and Pentecost. For the Orthodox Christian, there is no "dead time" nor even a *secular* calendar for his calendar is liturgical. He lives by its rhythm and immerses himself deeply in the atmosphere which is unique to each of the celebrated mysteries. The time of Advent does not have the same aroma as the time of Lent nor that of Pentecost. Throughout this new time, the Christian is purified from the old times of darkness; over the years he acquires, to his great surprise, a whole new sensitivity: the Sensitivity of Christ.

LIVING IN SONG

It must be understood that, in this radically different view of the sacraments, it is not a matter of adding sacred acts to profane ones. Worship is not an extension of life, but life itself placed at the heart of time in order to completely transform us from within. It is always the light which has come into the darkness (Jn 1). The Bible has always understood worship that way and, for this reason, Jewish mysticism has not only filled time with multiple benedictions, but has made it rhythmic to regular services throughout the day.

All this prepared for the coming of the Messiah and when God incarnated Himself, He made of time itself the sacrament of his Presence. That is why Jesus does not ask us to pray at particular times, but **"watch therefore, and pray always"** (Lk 21:36). Saint Paul insists in turn: "pray without ceasing" (1 Th 5:17), "with all perseverance" (Ep 6:18), "night and day" (1 Th 3:10). Conscious of the mysterious presence of Christ, in the very midst of their time, Christians have always sought a continual prayer (Ac 1:14). But to realize this incessant prayer, all the spiritual masters agree that we must begin with specific times, at fixed hours. These are "strong times" which continue to resonate throughout the other times, to create a spirit, a tonality all through the day. That is where perpetual prayer finds its axis. This is the birth of the "Divine Office" or the "Prayer of Hours": every three hours we sing "psalms, hymns and canticles" according to the precept of the Scriptures. And since it is always the same unique reality, to incorporate oneself into Christ, we celebrate all the great mysteries consecutively. Each day itself is a liturgical year, particularly the last three days of Holy Week. Even nighttime is celebrated as an office called "Nocturnals," which is a vigil of the spirit awaiting the divine Groom.

This two thousand year old tradition is not only meant for monks, but for every Christian. Such a life was easier in a rural civilization, as the rhythms of work were different. But even today many persons maintain the grand office of *Laudes* in the morning, *Vespers* in the evening, and sometimes the *Complies* at bedtime. Whatever the external possibilities may be to sing these services during the day, the principle must be kept if we wish to progress. As the first Christians often did, we can say the "Our Father" wherever we are and in whatever we are doing.

ETERNITY IN TIME

But this can be even more simplified: at certain hours or even at all hours, we can do a "remembering." This entails stopping every hour, even for a few seconds, to become conscious of oneself and to enter within: "to re-collect" oneself. Since our dispersion in the exterior, our multiple duties and concerns, our thousand worries and thoughts always express themselves in our body. From created tensions and superficial breathing from the chest, with shoulders raised and stomach held in a closed state . . . we must first release ourselves completely. We must then breathe deeply several times, straighten ourselves in good vertical posture, relax fully in the shoulders and re-center ourselves within our center of gravity, the stomach.

Simply putting ourselves in order physically can radically change our way of being centered and moves us instantly from distraction, disorder and incoherence to inner unity and presence. We are once again within ourselves, rooted, existing in the present moment. It will then be easy to become conscious of the One who inhabits this reconstructed time, to surrender ourselves into His hands and to offer Him the work that we are doing. "We need to let ourselves be filled with God's love for us and to marvel at it," which, according to Nicolas Cabasilas, is all that is necessary to become a saint.

This very short time, which does not interrupt our activities, has the brevity of lightning illuminating the darkness and like the drop of water falling regularly in the same spot: it digs into the rock and ends by splitting it. The characteristic of these times is that they bring us closer to the point where the whole day is lived in permanent recollection as though we saw "Him who is invisible" (He 11:27). This is a practice which results in great changes and within a few weeks we can already see some of the beautiful fruit of these efforts. These blessed moments open the vise of time which, without them, crushes us. They place us within the present moment which is their supreme essence. At that instant, we are, for "to be" is to be in the occurrence of each moment; it is the perception of the "Love and Plenitude of Being" where eternity and time cross each other in the present moment.

That is why the one who lives the present moment is always essentially in prayer, for the present is eternity in time; absence from the present is an invasive rupture and an alienation from our Source. Through the Presence, eternity enters into time; the more someone unites himself to Him, the more his being concentrates itself in the present. There is no more powerful asceticism than to live in the "here and now," in complete accord with the moment in which we find ourselves. This is the royal way of Obedience which is not servile submission but is the wedding of the human will to the Divine Will with total abnegation of our own will. This is the point of it all: to be in "each moment" here where God wants us to be and to receive the present moment as a gift from His hands. This is to live consciously and to inhabit even the smallest internal and external movements. The Christ consciousness then dwells within us. To be conscious of Him in all the parts of our being including the body, to taste His Presence in all experiences whether they please us or not, is ultimate personal consciousness and the summit of all joy.

FOCUSING ALL OF OUR ENERGIES ON A SINGLE POINT

But it is also the summit of asceticism to wish to consecrate oneself completely and exclusively to this effort. Every obstacle must be put aside, even our good excuses. To place oneself on the path with a divided will, with only a small fraction of one's energy and with mental hesitation, leads us nowhere! We must make a radical break with our habits and our way of being: Introducing to our inner selves through a decisive act which "shakes our whole nature to its foundations" a new idea-force; a total consecration of all our energies to the Divine Presence such that to live through Him becomes the only desire of our heart and the only ambition of our will. From this decision, all other desires and needs enter into a process of conversion and concentrate themselves in this consuming passion. This is not an intellectual concentration but a physical and spiritual awareness where everything is felt, seen and desired in the context of the Divine. The aim is to make every detail, every form of life, every incident and every movement into a sustenance to nourish the Divine Fire that inhabits us.

As long as we still live and act with egotistical motivations, we remain slaves of an inferior consciousness: we do not act for God but for our personal satisfaction and contentment. The Divine will not manifest Himself to us as long as we are seeking personal achievement. Our whole way of being, all of our actions, whether insignificant or profane, can and must be lived as sacred acts and in the consciousness of an offering to God. Everything must be directed toward Him, nothing must be undertaken only for ourselves and our other interests. Only in this way will the supports of the ego with its presence and influence be eliminated and all daily life focus on a single purpose. Behind everything there is the Presence and we must feel it always and everywhere, awakening to its constant intimate and enveloping existence within us, intensely perceiving it and communing with it in every moment. To turn all our emotions toward this Presence is the most intense means of purifying the heart. Sooner or later "the pure in heart will see God," will feel Him, touch Him, hear Him, breathe Him. All the senses, the limbs and vital functions will be invested with a Divine Light-Force which moves, feels and thinks within us (Acts 1:8).

Human beings are immersed in God. We can and will be one day, as was Saint Seraphim of Sarov, true sons and daughters of Light; but already from the beginning of the Path, during the most humble "call" in the midst of our activities, the seeker can make contact with this same Light. The same Light that inhabits the greatest of saints is also in our depths. At the beginning we only perceive it as a small vibration of silence in the background of our being; as the "rememberings" succeed one another, we realize that it is always there. This silence is a depth behind our consciousness and we can at will rest within it even in the midst of the daily tumult. We progressively become more sensitive to this immense silent ocean that vibrates deep within, this true Presence with which the rememberings ceaselessly reconnect and dialogue, and from which they pull up pails of living water as from a well.

As we advance, the intellect becomes quiet, and we progressively perceive that we no longer need to think or to speak in order to act. With the developed habit of constantly referring to the Presence within us, everything is given us at the instant it is needed and with infallible precision: without any reflection, the proper word surges forth. Everything without exception comes our way without effort, through silence of thought and will, and through complete submission to "the One who can do everything." It is an entirely different style of life, that of the Gospel, where action truly becomes contemplation. Whether such a person eats, works, or takes a walk, he remains rooted in the same Force which he lets pass through everything. This Force is the source of consciousness; nothing troubles it. Thoughts, images and even violent events can assail it without troubling its inner Peace.

We can only sense how far the "liturgicalization" of time and of our being can go. There are no limits to the joyous celebration of the Encounter in the "here and now," where we as priests of the Royal Priesthood restore the world to God as an offering. We make a temple of the world and a song of our life. "Bless the Lord, O my soul . . . I will sing to the Lord as long as I live; I will sing praise to my God while I have my being" (Ps 104)."I advance by singing you" (Saint John Climacus, seventh century).

OUR FIVE SENSES: WINDOWS OPEN ON THE INVISIBLE

The transformation of our being through liturgy, which is a true re-creation of ourselves, uses an utterly realistic and carnal teaching which is that of our five senses. The Fathers have always considered our senses as "windows open onto the invisible": God gave them to us to see Him, hear Him and touch Him. When separated from Him, they are, as we are, thrown into the exterior to seek interest in places other than in God. Liturgy will therefore take our senses where they are—on the exterior—and gradually reconfigure them to their original function.

1. THE MUTATION OF THE GAZE

The eyes assist with the veritable mutation of the gaze. The icons train the sight to a rigorous fasting and fill the eyes with the Divine Glory. Liturgy is for the eyes a sacred, grandiose theater; each color of the liturgical ornaments, differs according to the celebrated mysteries. Each color of the icons and frescos is a luminous vibration that will awaken in us an always deeper and unknown level of consciousness. The gaze becomes more and more internal.

There is no limit to the progress of this "ascending force" which makes of the saint a seer for whom everything is transparent. The aim of the liturgy is to reveal to us that the entire universe is a theophany, a manifestation of God who offers Himself in communion to those who know how to look and to contemplate. Every thing, all that exists is therefore a gift of the Invisible, everything including the most ordinary, opens onto infinite horizons. The sight of the contemplative becomes "heliomorphous," says Saint Gregory of Nyssea (fourth century): the light of his eyes is that of the Holy Spirit. The contemplative sees with "the eyes of the Dove" and recognizes that which is homogeneous to him, for the light which rests in his eyes is that very one which flows over all things. This is the presence of the Holy Spirit who makes us "see," for He is the Beauty that attracts us and calls to us, through this transparence, to contemplate the Word.

2. THE SOUND BEYOND SOUND

Hearing is certainly one of the most employed senses on the Path. Everything is sung in the liturgy, even the *readings*! The Judeo-Christian tradition has always known the role of the voice in the transformation of being. The voice is a mirror of the soul and that is why we recognize in it an irreplacable instrument for the knowledge of self and the exercise of spiritual development. The voice unveils to what extent its author is centered in his deep being or on the contrary is a prisoner of his surface self.

Thus, across the centuries of its history, the Church teaches the people to breathe through singing. The breath that animates us is the "breath of life" which God breathes into us (Gn 2:7). Therefore, there is nothing more important than to breathe consciously and in the right manner. Singing first relaxes us completely, liberates us from the tensions of our ego, and allows the exhalation to fulfill its tremendous function, as much on the psychosomatic level as on the spiritual one. At that moment, song will seize the human spirit and carry the singing Word beyond its audible limits. The song is the breath which introduces the Word into human hearts. This is the very nature of the liturgical song in relation to the aesthetic song. Its penetration is such that one day it sings within us as it breathes through us . . . The great breakthrough has occurred.

3. THE SCENT OF HOLINESS

The olfactory sense addresses the olfactive memory through the use of incense. The latter is always determined by its context which gives it a "subject." Incense by itself is merely a perfume. Used at the heart of the liturgy where we experience the divine mystery, we breathe the aroma of Christ. The organ of scent detects our sympathies and antipathies, and orients our desires. This is the primordial importance of incense at the heart of the mystic journey: it contributes to providing an axis to our chaotic impulses and turns desire into a Presence. Just as with song, the scent is inseparable from breathing; but here, breath can become so subtle that it recognizes Christ everywhere at the remembering of His particular aroma. And this aroma ends by penetrating the person himself, as the breath imbues his flesh and blood. This explains the "aroma of holiness" that we discover sometimes in the presence of great spiritual persons or even near their tombs. This union is the fruit of the gift of God to humanity and of humanity to God, the "sacrifice of praise," and expresses its magnitude in the psalm sung during the presentation of the incense: "May my prayer rise as incense before You."

4. TASTING HOW GOOD IS THE LORD

As we immerse ourselves in the liturgy's indescribable ambiance, there begins to be born within us the meaning of taste. It is at its height at the moment of communion. When there is nothing more to be said and the Ineffable visits us, we sing this psalm: "Taste and see how good is the Lord!" But little by little this new way of tasting manifests itself, settles in and remains with us even outside of the liturgy. It is as though another quality of perception has broken through the surface of our usual consciousness. Everything around us takes on a different flavor. As soon as we stop grasping everything conceptually, we are seized by their radiance, and rational interpretation no longer separates us from the immediate experience of the thing we are encountering.

This is one of the great goals of the liturgical teaching: it opens us to our depth and this allows us to also see other beings and things in their depth. We then discover what the specialists of the sacred call the "numinous," that superior quality which indicates to us, and relates to everything, the presence of another reality which is completely different from the one which is immediately before our five senses.

Teilhard de Chardin calls it "the diaphany of Being . . . the Universal Smile coming from the heart of all things . . . the first perceived shiver of the world animated by the incarnation of God." The Fathers of the desert designate it with this admirable expression: "the flame of things." At the center of the smallest object is unveiled the infinite immensity which contains everything. In the liturgy, when tasting the little parcel of bread, we learn that the infinite is in finite things and all eternity is in the passing second. That is why, as Saint Denys the Areopagite (sixth century) insists: "Man must unite himself to everything in order to liberate praise from mute nature." The liturgy is therefore a beginning without end.

5. ONLY CADAVERS FEEL NOTHING

The "touch" is a synthesizing and global sense. We touch or are touched through the five senses. But here it is the body in its entirety which is involved. As the "temple of the Holy spirit" (1 Co 6:19), our body is a place of initiation into the mysteries of Life and it is called to become transparent to Being which lies at its core in order to bear witness to Itself in the world. After His earthly mission,

Jesus did not say to his disciples: "Think of Me," but **"Handle Me!"** and "he breathed on them" (Lk 24:39 and Jn 20:22). In the liturgy, Christ dead and resurrected touches us entirely, constantly, and we touch Him, even into the intimacy of our breath. He breathes within us: "Flesh of my flesh, Blood of my blood!" cries out Saint Gregory Palamas (thirteenth century). We are infinitely closer to God through sense than through thought. Indeed, the Fathers tell us that the least thought, even about God, is an obstacle to encountering Him. "If God has slipped under my skin, it must be felt!" Saint Symeon (eleventh century) did not hesitate to say: "Is God nothing at all? For if He is something, those who are clothed with Him would have knowledge of this. It is when we put on nothingness that we feel nothing, while if we put on something we feel it quite clearly. Only cadavers feel nothing."

Long before him, Saint Isaac the Syrian (sixth century) said that "immortal life consists in feeling everything in God," and Saint Clement of Alexandria (second century) invited the first generations of Christians to "sense what God is through every sensation." This is the vitally important testimony of a tradition confronting the darkness of reason: "he who does not hear, does not see, and does not feel is spiritually dead" (Saint Gregory the Sinaite). From beginning to end, liturgy exercises the body so that it will let itself be touched by God and become physically conscious of His indwelling. Through the subtle detail of each of our senses we are always stimulated and maintained in a state of watchfulness; through deep relaxation which is openness and sensorial receptivity; through sung respiration, and finally through the great corporal attitudes—standing, sitting, kneeling or prostrated.

Through this continual touching, the body undergoes the apprenticeship of a way of being here which consists, according to Saint Paul, in "being rooted and grounded in Love" (Ep 3:17) and where, according to the word of Christ himself, we can have a depth of earth (Mt 13). This is what the Far East calls "Hara," a fundamental attitude which is omnipresent throughout the entire Bible and the Tradition.

A TEACHING THROUGH DIRECT OSMOSIS

The person whose life is punctuated by a regular liturgy and who introduces this same watchfulness in his daily life, knows that every action has two aspects. First, it is functional, i.e. we do something; and second, it is liturgical: God wants to manifest Himself through it. Realities as human as walking, sitting and standing can be divine. A liturgical being, someone who chooses to be on the Path, no longer peels potatoes in the same way. His daily life becomes exercise and every occasion is the best opportunity for advancing. Liturgy extends itself spontaneously.

Marcel Jousse, a contemporary Jesuit anthropologist, has shown us how (according to the coherence of the Incarnation of God in human flesh) this transformation was the very characteristic of the teaching of Jesus. Far from being a *knowledge*, it was a direct transmission by osmosis. After eight centuries of scholastic theology, we now need to rediscover everything. Liturgy is the place of this experience. The word and the gesture, says Jousse, are incorporated by the bones and the eardrum of the one who looks and who listens. Human beings mimic by nature and repeat, in microgestures at the core of our being, the gestures that we have seen or felt. Therefore, through *miming*, the gesture of the liturgical act becomes a part of the body which receives and, due to its irradiation, it literally incarnates itself in the body. This is the phenomenon called *intussusception* (from the Latin "to receive in our intimacy"), where we replay within us that which has touched us through our senses. We repeat "in echo," from the Greek *catecho* which gave us the word "catechism" and which was in the past done liturgically and not scholastically! It is a matter of total assimilation, in the most biological sense of the word, since this includes the eating of the Word in the Eucharist. The whole liturgy is an act of eating through the five senses which need to be in a state of constant receptivity. Then, as Saint Maximus the Confessor (seventh century) admirably expresses: "Through saintly participation in the pure and vivifying mysteries, man receives intimacy and identity with God: through it, man can obtain the possibility of becoming god out of the man that he was."

CHAPTER VI

PATHS OF HEALING

A NEW BIRTH

To live for the Divine Life, such as we have described it, one must first be born into it: **"Unless one is born of water and the Spirit, he cannot enter the Kingdom of God"** (Jn 3:5). This refers to baptism and its necessity is therefore absolute.

Such an affirmation is startling! What can three drops of water do in a human life when poured on the head of a baby in an obscure corner of a church? And yet this is the event which has not only given him life, but maintains him in it at every moment! To have completely forgotten it, to live as though it did not exist, is without doubt the most serious blow the demon can inflict upon us.

Baptism is not part of our unconscious past

169

definitively resolved, but is our current condition: we are that. In the early days of the Church, the preparation of an adult for baptism lasted three years. The forty days of Lent were understood as a veritable initiation through successive stages of the rite, culminating in baptism itself during the great night of Easter. There one immerged from the waters of an immense baptistry three times the person he had been. This experience enlightened the whole life of the first Christians and they were called "illumined ones." For them, baptism was the source of a permanent joy.

We are attempting to rediscover here and there the grandeur of this mystery. Orthodoxy has always safeguarded immersion, for "baptism" means "to be plunged in." The baptized plunge into Christ dead and resurrected, truly dying and being resurrected with Him. The baptismal water is Holy, it becomes the very presence of Christ and of the Holy Spirit through consecration, and through our faith the sacrament is accomplished.

Hearing these words of our death and resurrection, it is as though we had lost the ability that makes it possible for us to understand them because the concrete experience of these realities has disappeared. They are now merely gestures from another world, empty rituals and metaphors that leave us indifferent. But it is possible that we might recognize in this indifference the reality of our fall, of our existential separation from God: we are devoid of Life, and the proof is that we do not even understand its language. We can discover here the extent of a very real death that has settled within us. It is from this condition that baptism seeks to liberate us!

Christianity will be extinguished if it does not rediscover the vivid faith of our Fathers. For them, there was simply no life outside of Christ. Baptism was so central that it was lived as the very principle of the new birth, the re-creation of fallen humanity. This was not "symbolic" or "metaphorical" but rather the biological transformation of human beings. Nicolas Cabasilas, layman of the fourteenth century, has admirably reintroduced the faith of this Tradition in his book whose title alone sums it up: *Life in Christ*.

Christ is the prototype of the human being. We are created in His image and must conform to Him. Outside of Christ, then, we are nothing but chaos, we are unformed matter. Cabasilas is very realistic in his description: when we pour a metal such as gold into a mold, it takes the shape of a gem or a statue. So man, "formless matter," is poured into the water of baptism and comes out of it dressed with the beauty of Christ, "modeled and conformed." This is an actual ontological mutation in which Christ resurrected, uniting His energies with the baptized, transmits His own senses and Divine faculties. "Rising out of the water, we carry the Savior Himself in our souls, on our head, in our eyes, in our entrails, on our limbs and pure from sin, freed from all blemish, such as the resurrected One is . . . "

Cabasilas insists that Christ "corporally" penetrates within us and therefore our transformation is "biological" and "psychosomatic." Our faculties are those of the Body of Christ, "just as iron plunged into the fire becomes fire itself (molten) and keeps nothing of the iron." Therefore, "when Christ melts within us, He changes us and transforms us into Him . . . All the spiritual faculties immediately fuse, soul with Soul, body with Body and blood with Blood." There is nothing left of the old man as Saint Paul states, because "we were buried with Him through baptism into death, that just as Christ was raised from the dead by the glory of the Father, we also should walk in newness of life . . . we shall be in the likeness of His resurrection" (Ro 6:4-5).

For the baptized, life is now Christ: "It is no longer I who live, but Christ lives in me" (Ga 2:20). The person is integrally remodeled in his nature and in his personhood, in the most intimate part of himself.

From then on, the first Christians knew that they were no longer the same, their way of being in the world and of understanding life had become radically different. Their whole being was now re-oriented: their fundamental attitude, the motives of living and decision-making, the solution of all their problems and the little details of their daily lives found their source and light exclusively in this baptism. The Acts of the Apostles are a resplendent manifestation of this fact. The baptismal commitment of these Christians was unconditional and their joyous consciousness of being resurrected was such that to "die" physically under persecution was looked upon "as a gain" (Ph 1:21). In those days, thousands sang as they entered the arenas. Christ alone was their Lord and their faith challenged all systems and structures.

It is of the highest urgency for each person individually

and for the Church as a whole to rediscover the power of this sacrament which is the foundation of life. On the personal level, baptism becomes "burning" with authenticity for us, as for the first Christians, through the Eucharist. If baptism "immerses" us in Christ to clothe us in Him (Ga 3:27), the Eucharist "assimilates" us increasingly into Him. Then, as Cabasilas states: "Through these sacred signs, we live, we move and we are." Our consciousness as baptized persons, as awakened ones, is our single and true condition, transcending all the other conditionings of our existence. Life itself becomes an arena in which we enter each morning to offer a joyous death to the One who has already resurrected us.

From an early age, the Orthodox child receives this abundance of Life through his baptism and the Eucharist. In the Orthodox tradition, the baby indeed communes with the Body and Blood of Christ as soon as he is baptized. The divine life flows in him, structures and builds him, just as nutrition, gestures of tenderness, language and culture construct him on other levels. It is God who chooses the person first (Jn 15:16), then when the time of maturity has come, the individual, in full consciousness, is called to say "yes" or "no."

There are more and more lay persons today who are becoming conscious of all this and are helping the Church to rediscover the truth of this developmental ritual. It is not difficult to ask the celebrant of a baptism to receive total immersion, and if there is no baptistery, to use a barrel as Saint Remi did with Clovis in the fifth century. He can be asked to participate in the exorcism which removes evil at its root, the solemn renunciation of Satan. The inbreathing of the breath of Life as was done at the creation of humanity (Gen 2:7), the anointing of the body with oil as a sign of burial with Jesus, and finally the rite of denudation which symbolizes the fall of the "old garments" of skin is thorough. Now the donning of the white tunic represents the innocence of "paradise regained" and flowing with the Glory of God. Once again, the human being is dressed with the royal mantle, he is king of creation which in its entirety is now the living sacrament of Jesus Christ, outside of which nothing can have any meaning.

THE INNER MASTER

That which is offered to us through baptism and the

Eucharist is made possible because of the Holy Spirit. It is He who vivifies these mysteries within us each time we open ourselves to them. Also, it is through the power of the Spirit that the death and resurrection of Christ transcend time and are made actual for us today. We can become conformed to Christ and resemble Him, but it is only through the Holy Spirit that this can be done. There is no baptism or Eucharist, nor even a spiritual path without the sacrament of the Spirit, known as "chrismation" or "confirmation." These three inseparable sacraments are given during the Christian initiation, and they are called (from the beginning) the sacraments of initiation.

All of this has become only empty words in our day. Our mentality has become ritualistic and magical through our attitude toward these sacraments. We have rejected them or cast suspicion on them "because they bring us nothing, nothing takes place when we receive them, we are the same afterward as before." Our own judgement condemns us, for in order to receive a gift, do we not have to extend our hand? Can the rays of the sun shine through a dirty window? On the Path, it is not only the hand, but our whole being which must offer itself, open itself, become transparent and become a receptive cup.

To die with Christ, we must wish it, and not only during the rite, but in every moment of our lives; to be dressed in the splendor of His resurrection, we must leave behind our soiled clothing and purify ourselves. This is an exclusive and total commitment which cannot be only one among others. We should not give to God only a little of our time, on Sunday at service, leaving the rest of the week to ourselves! **"Let your yes be yes and your no, no . . . Who is not with Me is against Me . . . "** Jesus cuts with these words as with a sword. The person who does not extend to his entire life the sacrament received in church through a decisive and relentless struggle (gambling all his cards on that which must become the only axis of his life) would be better off not receiving the sacraments at all. He consumes them for his perdition, like Prometheus who stole the fire from heaven for his own satisfaction.

The sacrament of chrismation is precisely the gift of the Spirit "everywhere present and filling everything." This presupposes that we open all the closed doors of our existence to Him! This is a true personal Pentecost, and the fire of the Spirit descends on us as it did on the Apostles.

That is why we use the holy "chrism" for chrismation: the oil is capable of incandescence and as such symbolizes the light which gives fire, the purity through fire which burns completely, for fire penetrates everything as does the oil. An oil stain on paper penetrates it through and through, takes possession of it and makes it transparent; the paper then carries the mark in its very fabric and its structure. This extraordinary plenitude of oil overflows and enters in external life through the fruits of fecundity and joy. These are the very ways of the Holy Spirit Himself!

When a person offers himself to the Spirit, He fully possesses him. The newly baptized receives the anointing of the holy chrism over his entire body: the forehead, the eyes, the ears, the nostrils, the lips, the chest, the hands and feet, while the priest says each time: "The seal of the gift of the Holy Spirit." As a seal imprints its form, the Spirit indeed "in-forms," makes the form of Christ penetrate within us. Throughout history, the seal marks a person or an object as the indisputable property of the one whose imprint he carries and whose protection is theirs by the same right. The baptized is "sealed" by the Holy Spirit, he no longer belongs to himself, neither does his life nor all that he touches. There is no longer a sacred and a profane for him, all the walls have fallen and the Presence is universal. He is always inspired by the Spirit, and "he overflows with an inexpressible joy because the Spirit of God transforms into joy all that it touches," says Saint Seraphim of Sarov (nineteenth century).

In other words: everything can become a place and a moment of revelation, for at the heart of all life He is the Life, He is the Presence behind all joy and all love, and it is His face which is manifested within all beauty. To live is to seek Him and to love Him through everything; to find Him is to no longer have any lack or any other desire, for His coming is the fulfillment of true happiness. He makes of every encounter an epiphany where two beings are sealed by the glory of God, He makes of each thing a Burning Bush where the encounter with the Divine is possible. To live in this way is to be in the Kingdom, as Christ lived it. The Holy Spirit is the very Spirit of Christ from all eternity. As Jesus lived everything on earth under the impulse of the Spirit, so it is with us now (Ga 5:25). The true disciple of Christ does not make any decision without the Holy Spirit. He cannot still engage his freedom in an autonomous

179

fashion, knowing that he could lose life itself, emptying it of its content. We can see that it is clearly in the "here and now" that the so-called "spiritual" (that is, according to the Spirit) life is realized!

In the Old Testament, all the kings, priests and prophets received the anointing of oil. But it was only a prefiguration of the Oil par excellence, the Messiah, who is King, Priest and Prophet in person. Immersed in Him during baptism and anointed by the power of the Spirit, we are kings "in His image." God has entrusted the earth as a kingdom (Gen 1:26), and has entrusted royalty on our everyday life. That is where, in the depths of our heart, being king over the empire of our passions, the world either perishes or is preserved in each person. It is here in the world that we open it anew to its Beyond for which it was created.

In bringing the world back to God, we are also priests, we exercise a royal priesthood, we make of the world and of all creation a place of communion with God! To turn the world away from this goal was humanity's worst betrayal and its fall. To take the world as an end in itself, cut off from God, makes of it a hellish ruin.

We are king of creation in order to be its benefactor, we are priest in order to offer it to God and we are prophet through this holy anointing. Contrary to popular belief, the prophet is not a diviner or someone who predicts the future: the prophet sees God everywhere present and hears His word at the heart of time, in any event or situation. Instead of a horizontal reading of history, he reads it prophetically, in its depths where he discerns and deciphers the will of the Creator who is always at work. Impassioned with God, the prophet sees everything in its Divine transparence. It is as though he has antennaes to receive even the smallest impulse of the Spirit in order to transmit it to the world. He is the witness of the Beyond in the depths of every present reality and the prophet shakes our sloth which has "no eye to see or ears to hear." Every person should naturally hear the voice of God and dialogue with Him, for the chrismic anointing restores every one of us anew in this faculty.

It is in this triple ministry as king, priest and prophet (our true vocation) that we build the world and give birth to a new humanity called "Church", the "race of the twice born," the Body of Christ and Temple of the Holy Spirit:

this is the realization in this world of the Kingdom of God. We can clearly see how the three sacraments are intimately related and how they "initiate" us to a new life. Renewed from top to bottom in our being, through baptism and anointing, we can sit at the eucharistic banquet with our brothers and sisters and become with them the Body of Christ. Becoming a community once again united with its Creator, belonging to "the household of God" (Ep 2:19) and drawing the whole of humanity into its movement toward the life of the Resurrected One. Any other meaning given to the Church is perverse. The Church is Eucharist and the Eucharist is the Sacrament of sacraments. The members of this new human community are not better or more virtuous than others, but they are born anew and their life is ontologically different.

LIGHT ON THE PATH

Through the three sacraments of Christian initiation, Jesus Christ has accomplished everything within us, and it is up to us to accomplish everything in Him. This is our Path and on this Path, as Christ Himself says, we fall seven times a day, that is, ceaselessly. Along this path we truly experience day after day, in the abyss of our failures, what it means to be separated from God. We constantly betray the great love God has for us, and to see inspite of everything, His arms always open to receive us anew. For this immense work of clearly seeing ourselves, of awakening and deepening our consciousness, of forgiveness and of an always more decisive rooting in God, Christ gives us the sacrament of "penitence". Through this act, the spiritual Path with its ups and downs, and the present moment within the density of daily life, asceticism and mysticism become sacrament. With penitence we always have with us on this Path the spiritual Master, the invisible Companion who accompanies us. Along the way, we place our steps in His, every fall sends us into His open arms on the cross and He saves us from our failures. There is no hell in which He has not descended if we open our eyes to see Him, there is no situation from which He does not seek to pull us out, if we are willing to give Him our hand. The "sacrament of penitence" is nothing but that, always and again returning to Christ in whom baptism has definitely plunged us, but Whom we constantly betray. The Path is long, painful, and impossible to live through alone.

To say that we have reduced the immensity of this sacrament to an admition of faults in a confessional (to a legal power which redresses our wrongdoings before the law) or, in the best of cases, to a spiritual conversation is to have misunderstood Christ's intention for us on the human Path. It is therefore not surprising that this sacrament has nearly disappeared and has left only a few traces in the practice of general absolution. If certain Christians rediscover its importance today, it is because they have become conscious of their lives as baptized persons. The sacrament of penitence is indeed a baptism, reconciliation after betrayal, a new death and a new resurrection: we are once again grafted onto Christ and his Body, the Church, after having been separated.

That which specifically relates this sacrament to baptism is its direct link to the Path, to our very personal evolution where discernment of the Spirit at work within us is critical. Most of the time we confuse fault and sin, which is a great obstacle on the Path. Each one of us carries within a kind of image to which we seek to correspond and, not achieving it, we feel terribly guilty. But this has nothing to do with the motives of sin, for guilt is the antithesis of the Gospel: it is disappointed pride. Sin, being our separation from God, our Source of Life, is an illness characteristic of the death of the soul. Only God can heal us from it and give us Life. Through the sacrament of penitence the Holy Spirit infuses the saving Christ within us Who recreates the soul, vivifies it, and then "restores it" fully in the Eucharist. The person who regularly practices this passage from death to life through the sacrament of penitence knows how much his soul is overwhelmed by it every time. At first there is always a resistance within because the ego knows that it is going to die, to be humiliated and unmasked, but later we are invaded by the amazing joy of resurrection, a sensation of freedom, and our whole being is in celebration (Lk 15:23-24).

Contrary to what we often believe, confession is not a punctual act, a sacrament which we receive several times a year. Confession, which is both a culmination and a new beginning, begins with a clear gaze upon oneself that must be done with precision and occur daily, becoming little by little a state of permanent watchfulness. There is no spiritual life without this time in which, every evening, we examine the life we are leading, to appreciate it in the light of Christ. This is not an analysis, but an orientation of our whole being toward the one necessary question: how is Christ present in my life? What are the constant inclinations of my heart, my deepest desires? Is my life leading somewhere?

Ultimately there is only one question, the one of love: **"Love one another. By this all will know you are My disciples"** (Jn 13:35). Christ is present there where our freedom affirms itself and opens onto love. After having prayed, for it is only by approaching God that we discover how far we are from Him, we must simply study the day that has gone by: how have I loved or not loved in today's situations, encounters, or events? Is it truly love that motivates my behavior and reactions? It is in the course of this effort that we really learn to give thanks: by being amazed every night at the actions of grace in each moment of our day! God is always present, even when we are sinning, and His constant Love, which "nothing can separate us from" (Ro 8:39), also reveals to us our sin. We discover then, not in guilt but in the infinite tenderness of God, how we have "missed the mark" (the exact translation of the word "sin"), how the meaning of our life in its deepest orientation, has been derailed: "I have lived as though God did not exist, I have betrayed His Love. I see this simply, and I recognize it without judgement." Day after day discernment is refined, rising out of imprecision and vagueness which is the drama of our spiritual life. God shows us how this love between "He and I" has taken place today minute after minute through very specific acts. And the day will come when we will understand through experience how in each moment of our life, we have the incredible power to please God or to displease Him! There are no "venial" or "mortal" sins, small or great ones: for those who love each other, nothing is insignificant, and to separate oneself from God is always deadly. He alone has Life. When a stream is cut off from its source, it immediately loses its identity and becomes a stagnant pool. So it is with human beings.

Real consciousness of sin is terrible: Christ dies from it and the saints have spilled torrents of tears over their treason. It is important that we also weep. Sometimes our eyes shed tears, other times it is only our heart that cries. Whatever the case may be, when we weep our affective depth is touched by the process of conversion and that is what is crucial. Tears purify us like the water of baptism and immerse us in the death of the old man. But under these same tears will appear the smile of the resurrection and they will become tears of joy. "The greater the repentance, the shorter the Path," said Father Sophrony.

This progressive purification gives direction to our rebirth. Through the clear and regular gaze upon oneself, our multiple desires are "tested," as metal is tested by fire, and unite little by little around the same axis: our vocation. At the end of a certain length of time, we see our inner unity emerge. Ultimately, there is only one desire: the Unique Desired One. There is only one true weakness, but it inscribes itself in the concrete and personal details of our lives: nothing is more important than to discover in what way this occurs! He who comes to know his greatest weakness also knows on what point his spiritual effort will have the maximum intensity. The rallying point of our energies focuses our whole being in a fundamental attitude that makes it possible for us to experience an active relationship with God and His work within us. Our response to God's incessant call, **"Come, follow Me"** (Lk 18:22), is our very life. The present moment becomes the place, the time and the means of our progress: "We will understand everything some day," said Emmanuel Mounier, "in the meantime, let us grow through that which happens to us."

Therefore, what is in the beginning a punctual exercise can later become an almost continuous state which is called watchfulness or "the watch of the heart." This is the whole aim of the Path and one of the greatest graces that God can give us in this life.

From this journey, which is often a painful battle, comes the act of confession itself. It renders the whole effort sacramental, that is to say, we are accompanied by the Divine Presence and Power. To admit one's greatest weakness, one's sin, before God through the intermediary of a priest, who is the witness to Christ and to the whole ecclesiastical community, is to undergo "a veritable surgical operation" (M. A. Costa de Beauregard, *Suffering and obedience according to the Fathers*). To tear something away from oneself, such as a passion with which we have identified ourselves, is truly a death, a crucifixion which is impossible to accomplish by oneself. All those who call upon psychotherapists know this well. It escapes our human power, and that is why it is a sacrament through which the power of the Holy Spirit intervenes. The person who expresses his sin in confession climbs onto the cross with Christ through a voluntary death. This can cause incredible suffering if the preparation is authentic, but the sacrament saves this humiliated person who, instead of identifying himself with his wrongdoing, identifies with Christ. Dead to death, this person no longer dies: he is already resurrected.

The only way for us not to die is to freely accept to live death here and now, as Christ has shown us. Confession then becomes a spiritual event with unsuspected impact: what could have been the end of the individual is metamorphosized into definitive and eternal Life through the power of Christ's resurrection and His love. Sin separates us from everything: from God, from our brothers, from ourselves, from the world and from life itself; now, because we have been able to speak of it at the heart of the sacrament, the Word —Christ dead and resurrected—turns separation into communion.

This love of Christ is concretely applied in the life of the one who confesses through remedies that the priest gives him for the healing of his soul. Faced with his wrong, the priest advises him on an attitude of new life. This will be a precious instrument for his daily self-observation and the watch of the heart. Then, at the end of confession, the person seized by the desire for forgiveness and repentance, receives the imposition of the hands from the priest, the gesture of Christ and the descent of the Spirit. At that moment, the sinner is freed from his sins for they are utterly annihilated and absorbed in the passion of Christ. The person who rises from this creative act is no longer the same, he feels the divine energies flowing within him. **"Enter into the joy of your Lord"** (Mt 25:21) and the whole of heaven rejoices with Him (Lk 15:7). His life has become celebration and he can let thanksgiving surge forth which always puts the Christian in his true tonality. He was disconnected by the sadness of sin, and the joy of resurrection places him back in his "normal" dimension. Only praise can maintain him in this perfect harmony, for it depends on God alone and quiets all the false notes of sin. "Go tell the Christians that they have only one duty in the world: Joy!" (Paul Claudel).

I RETURN TO YOU

Sin, which is separation from God who is Life, inevitably leads to death through suffering and illness. Far from God, all humanity is sick and gives birth only to die. We come into the world condemned to death. It is not for this horror that God created us! He is Plenitude of Life and can only give plenitude and "life in abundance" (Jn 10:10). It is we who have fallen, who never cease to separate ourselves from God and who live as though He did not exist. We therefore introduce death in all that we do, time itself becomes death-dealing and devours every instant of our existence.

"Suffering and death" is only the announcement of our final destruction. Death, present everywhere and always, is the great adversary of humanity; death is our enemy. The secularized societies, no longer knowing the Bible and the motives of death, try today to tame it, to civilize it and give it a normal status. Numerous books on the after-life take the drama out of reality, seeking to minimize the panic, anguish, and the tragedy of the situation. But nothing works, for where would this sudden increase of life come from? No human help or book holds the keys to this life.

The answer is in God alone. He made Himself humanity to save us from death and to heal our wounds. Today, He is also with us, in the most intimate history of each individual. The Church is His very Presence and the sacraments are His hands that touch us and heal us. In the Gospel, we see Jesus healing all the sick: the paralyzed, the blind, the deaf, the lepers, the epileptics, the possessed. The Apostles continued the same action: "They cast out many demons, and anointed with oil many who were sick and healed them" (Mk 6:13). Christ pursues these healings down through the centuries to the end of time. He is in the midst of humanity as Savior, as Giver of life. It is He who is always and everywhere at work: in nature and in plants, in medicine and in therapies, in all the energies of the human body. There is no healing outside of Him, just as there is no water without a source! He is the Life, even of those who ignore everything about Him or deny Him.

But the sacrament of the sick introduces us into an entirely new dimension. In the past, this sacrament was "administered" only once: at the moment of death; and when the priest came to the house, everyone knew that "it wouldn't last much longer!" The sacrament was called "extreme unction" and it was held off to the last moment, often to the point where the sick person was no longer conscious of it. His loved ones did not want to terrify him! No one hoped for healing from this final rite. Today, when we ask so many questions concerning death, it is not surprising that we are rediscovering the splendor of this sacrament. The anointing of the sick is destined for all, whatever the physical or psychic gravity of his state. We can receive this sacrament as often as necessary; it infallibly begins the healing process, otherwise Christ would only be an impostor, a useless "savior."

Usually, we only understand the word "healing" in a limited way, as the disappearance of a symptom, but the sacrament seeks to heal the whole person: body-soul-spirit, to eradicate the cause of the illness at its very root. That is why the sacrament also concerns the journey of the person and not only a particular illness which he may have temporarily acquired. Since the source of all life is found in the return toward God, the sacrament will first decontaminate the sick by offering divine forgiveness to the patient. Healing in depth is linked to repentance, for separation from God is the only obstacle to life in plenitude. The objectivity of the sacrament manifests the fact that complete forgiveness on the part of God is always offered to us as soon as we attempt even the slightest movement toward Him. The greatest crimes, then, such as those of the thief crucified next to Christ, "are only a handful of sand in the ocean of infinite love" (Saint Isaac the Syrian).

Through anointing, this person is healed in the depth of his being, where the illness originates. He may be healed physically and psychically, or he may die, at which point death itself will be transformed by the sacrament into the greatest remedy for eternal healing. There is nothing magical in this, they are stages on the journey of our life, and the sacrament is there to give life its unexpected scope. In no case does it take the place of the doctor or medicine when they are unsuccessful. On the contrary: it inserts them into the great movement of the life of the person where everything is sanctified. This includes illness and suffering and all that is a part of the path of healing.

The aim of the sacrament of the sick is the following: the metamorphosis of evil, which is suffering, into good whatever the outcome of this suffering may be. Through the sacrament, Christ Himself enters into our suffering and it is He who lives it in us and through us. A complete reversal then takes place: the illness or the suffering which were obstacles to life, can become the very place of the the most intimate communion with God, a place where life manifests itself differently and in plenitude. This can occur to such an extent that the very ill are often witnesses of a surprising faith and much more "alive" than their visitors who are in "good health."

The grace of the sacrament introduces us into the very attitude of Christ during his Passion in Gethsemane. We ask God to heal us: **"O My Father, if it is possible, let this cup pass from Me."** At the same time this prayer is immediately fulfilled by leaping into the right attitude: **"Nevertheless, not as I will, but as You will"** (Mt 26:39). Our free decision to accept the unacceptable is always "initiatory," that is, it opens the doors of mystery within us and leads us toward a transcendence of appearances. Through anointing this acceptance is clothed with a sacramental configuration to Christ and our life enters into a process of transmutation which has no concern with opposites, health or sickness, suffering or well-being, life or death. At the very heart of the opposites that daily life brings us constantly, there is an "essential" dimension of life through which we can be definitively healed on a level other than the physical or psychic ills. Prior to external healing, which is always possible and often granted, this anointed person remains totally indifferent, he sometimes even refuses help, knowing now a plenitude of life incomparable to all that he or she has experienced before.

The whole life of Christ initiates us to this way of being in every moment, even if our illness is not in an acute phase. It is nevertheless in critical periods that we accept more easily, though painfully, a fundamental requirement of faith. When nothing is going right in the eyes of human beings, in the greatest darkness of our passion, Christ shows before the world and history the only possible path beyond suffering. The only answer to a question that humanity has never been able to answer: the acceptance of the unacceptable because the Will of God is expressed there. This is faith in its purest state since nothing keeps us from believing! And this total and fully confident surrender, in which nothing remains of our own will, allows

God to act with power, to make of suffering and even of death a veritable alchemy. As the chrysalis enclosed in its shell becomes a butterfly, so we are transformed into the fullness of resurrection.

This configuration to the Easter of Christ was the fundamental attitude of the disciples. Peter, James and John, the three great initiated ones, were the first to receive it in the intimacy of Christ suffering at Gethsemany. It is the attitude of the child in the hands of the Father, not only in suffering, but in each moment, since each moment is a trial "testing" us "as iron in the fire" to verify our faith. Whether in bad times, in the thousand troubles of the day, in illness or death, only the "yes" without reservation to every event, every situation and every moment takes us out of sin, out of our separation from God. We are one with God and life's events as the child is one with its mother, surrendered into her arms. Nailed on the cross, Christ is the Child *par excellence*, **"Father, into Thy Hands I commit My Spirit."** And He immediately adds, since now the secret of right attitude has been given to his disciples: **"It is finished!"**

Only this total acceptance, this total surrender, this

"yes" without reservation to all that happens (with the conviction that God is acting and never ceases to create) makes Christ victorious over suffering and death instead of being vanquished by them. God has entered into history, descending right into the thickness of our human experience, and especially into suffering, death and even hell. This makes all our hellish situations, as well as the ordinary fabric of our daily lives the place of our encounter with Him. Our acceptance is the place of the Covenant; it is precisely where the exchange of wills occurs between God and the individual. Following Christ who is completely "Yes" (2 Co 1:19), we pronounce our "yes" by surrendering to the circumstance, letting ourselves be crucified on the situation offered to us: **"Thy will be done!"** Then from the event, as revolting as it may be for the ego, comes "the glory of God" as Saint Paul said. Since "we have resisted to the blood " we are in turn the "Lamb," just as Christ was, and suffering is transmuted into the "Marriage of the Lamb."

Christ revealed to us that we can love suffering because it makes us similar to Him, and in so doing He liberates us from it. God has a perfect plan for history, and our work is to commune with it. The sacrament of anointing offers us this constant communion. We are here in the presence of a radically new approach to our daily life: it is a revolutionary way of being at the heart of the pain of existence, a complete conversion of our usual attitude. The sacrament of the sick introduces us into the Kingdom of heaven where physical and psychic healing, even if it takes place, is very little compared to the illumination which it provides for us.

I WILL WED YOU TO MYSELF FOREVER

The only true vocation of human beings is to love; this vocation contains all the others and without it they lose their value. Everything will pass away, but love alone will not pass away; it is the only earthly reality which will remain eternally. The only reality which deserves to be known and propagated, the only one which makes human beings ill when they lack it and the only one which heals us and fills us with happiness when we have it. For love is God Himself. In reality, there is only one path, the path of love: if we are "made in the image of God," it means that in our depths we are love and our destiny is always to love more in order to perfect our love.

A human being is only truly human if he or she becomes god; we experience divinization only by love and it is only through love that we become disciples. Every other path leaves us in the animal sphere and we do not realize our unsuspected potential lying dormant within. Only love reaches our depths! To live is to love. Love is the illumination and saintliness of humanity. Each one of us is called to this state and every moment has meaning or plenitude only through this state. I can know and possess all the secrets of human power, but if I "have not love, I have become sounding brass or a clanging cymbal" (I Co 13:1).

Marriage is therefore not a "biological fatality" nor a "remedy to concupiscence," still less is it a consecraton of the family which has nothing evangelical about it but is often only a middle class perversion of love. Marriage is meant to be the very sacrament of the Covenant between God and His entire Creation. If God is Love, He can only be ecstacy, reaching outside of Himself with the desire to make His creatures participate in His life of love. It is therefore a covenant in the strongest sense of the term, a conjugal union and wedding that God seeks with us. The whole Bible speaks of this Divine-human revelation in nuptial terms, and this mutual gift of "Lovers" culminates in an eternal wedding (Rev 19:7). In the "fullness of time," the coming of the Messiah will be the visible manifestation of the face of Beauty to his spouse—humanity—who "languishes for her Beloved" every day of its long history. Christ comes to reveal to us that God Himself is fullness of communion, and therefore the source of communion: Three in One.

In creating humanity, God has deposited in our heart the imprint of His own loving existence. That is why all that animates us, all that we do from morning till night finds love to be its secret purpose. We never cease to aspire toward something unknown and we fill this yearning in a thousand ways, but our heart will find rest only in God.

When two beings love and wed each other in God, they are the great sign of all this, of humanity's wedding with God. The "Yes" through which we give ourselves reciprocally was first the "yes" of Mary. Through Mary, humanity takes a new path; she is the "Beloved" announced in the Song of Songs, "sick with love" (5:8); it is she who "draws us after her" (1:4) and thanks to her the "winter" of humanity "is passed" (2:11), and "the flowers appear on the earth" (2:12). Limitless love is once again possible: "for love is strong as death, many waters cannot quench love, neither can floods drown it" (8:6-7). All history is in balance around Mary's "Yes," and humanity becomes a receptive cup, receiving God in its entrails. Mary offers her flesh and her blood so that they might become, in this wedding, the flesh and blood of God. It is the first Eucharist where God becomes human so that we may become god. We "assimilate" each other and "melt" into Him through an unbreakable covenant. This "new and definitive" covenant is now offered to all humanity and the place of its realization will be the Eucharist until the end of time, **"when I drink it new with you in My Father's Kingdom"** (Mt 26:29). Through the Eucharist, we become Mary, become the Church, humanity on the path. When, as Mary, we recover our direction toward God, we become virgin, coming out of the multiple and "wedding" a single Source. The "conjugal bed" of this wedding between God and humanity is the Eucharist: a fusion without confusion, communion, carnal reciprocity, a true "blend" according to the powerful expression of Saint Gregory of Nyssea (fourth century).

From this we begin to understand in what perspective we must place the "sacrament of love" which is called marriage. Through the Eucharist every person, whether monk, celibate in the world or married, moves toward the wedding of all humanity with God. The Church has no other reason for being than to offer a "place" where this is possible: giving to each person his or her personal path and the concrete means for responding to this universal vocation which is divinization.

Only the sacrament, lived as spiritual path, lifts marriage out of the pure fatalism of the animal need for procreation. "There is a deplorable seriousness," wrote Kierkegaard (the Danish philosopher of the nineteenth century), "which consists in marrying, having children, contracting gout, taking exams, becoming a deputy . . . " Indeed, God did not create us for such a living death!

Marriage receives its plenitude from the Eucharist. Until the ninth century, there was no particular rite to unite husband and wife; the simple fact of participating in the

Eucharist was the sacrament of their love. And today still, in the rebirth of Orthodoxy in the West, we do not think of marriage outside of the liturgy, for that is where it finds its substance: only the goodness of God who dies of love for us can be the source of all nuptual love and make it stronger than death. The union of the beloved is inextricably linked to the Easter of Christ, and their wedding is the celebration throughout their journey of the "Marriage of Lamb" with humanity.

It is not by accident that Christ opened His path, the "Hour" of His Easter, and "manifested His glory" during the wedding at Cana (Jn 2:1-12). It is at this marriage that the messianic age announced by the prophets begins. Christ descends into the human love of man and wife, makes Himself present to them, and this sacrament transforms the water of their natural passion into the wine which symbolizes the mystic intoxication of perfect love. It can only be perfect through the total gift of self toward which Christ will lead them, when the Hour opened at Cana culminates in the Hour of the Last Supper where He transforms the wine into blood and the blood into the fire of the resurrection. The couple that assimilates this

Eucharist is in turn transformed into a "single flesh" and this flesh is that of Christ Himself. Their love is sealed by the Flesh and Blood of God.

That is why Saint John Chrysostom (fourth century) speaks here of the "sacrament of love," for "love changes the very substance of things," it is a permanent miracle, a metamorphosis, the mystical way through one's own existence. The true lover is inevitably a contemplative: if God dwells corporally in the other, then he can see in her the invisible Beauty, the radiance of His Glory and can touch the Untouchable. There, the embrace of the two lovers is in reality the embrace of Fire. No place else do we find such a thrill as in this communion from being to being that opens onto the infinite of Divine Love. The fruit of this union is not primarily the birth of a child, but the rebirth of the two lovers on a completely different level of consciousness, which is proof of the possibility of another humanity.

The lovers are priests of this permanent transmutation. The Eucharist which their conjugal priesthood celebrates is inscribed in the fabric of daily life, where every difficulty can be thrown into the furnace of love. This is a spiritual path that assumes a rough battle and an asceticism that is as challenging as that of the monks! In the Orthodox rite, we crown the husband and wife at the end of the celebration of the sacrament. They are "crowned with glory and honor," certainly, but also with their Master's crown of thorns and that of the martyrs. There is no love without the cross: to love without accepting to die for the other is to love only oneself. The spirituality of the couple is easy to express: to seek the joy of the other, to learn to say "You"! But it is a tomb for the ego, and at the same time it is the discovery of supreme happiness. In this, the lovers are an icon of the Trinity itself, where One says "You" to the Other in making it live and in entering into total abnegation.

To die from loving is the only way to love. Marriage is the path of this unconditional love, it does not depend on external circumstances, it is free, it is the path that Saint John said was God Himself. On this path, the lovers become "companions of eternity," tearing each other away from the daily limitations, breaking through absurdity and nothingness toward a beyond where life begins to dance. This love is a "road of saintliness," for those who love each other are of the race of God and they invite all of humanity to their wedding.

I COME TO DO YOUR WILL

If there are priests in the Church, it is only to remind the people at every moment that they are a priesthood, that the life of each person is a liturgy leading the journey toward the Kingdom. The priest is there to awaken human beings to their unique vocation "to love" and he offers them the methods of this path. In other words: there is no priestly cast in the Church and the priest has no specific vocation. He is the one who presides at the heart of the "priestly people" and who presents their gifts to God. He immolates himself for the community so that it may live from the love of Christ. His abnegation must be such that it is truly Christ who offers Himself through his ministry.

This sacrifice finally assimilates the priest to Christ Himself in His Easter: it is a sacrificial life, but for the joy of the world. The priest is nothing and, if he has a will of his own, his priesthood ceases to exist by that very fact. On one hand he identifies himself with Christ whose actions he expresses in the midst of the people, and on the other hand he identifies himself with the people whom he leads toward God. Completely stripped, the priest becomes sacrament in his very being: he communicates the Presence of Christ. As long as as something of himself still interposes itself, he is an obstacle to the reign of God and he betrays his Master.

Christ has said: **"Who has seen Me, has seen the Father"**; the priest should be able to say, if he dared: "Who sees me, sees Christ." The mystery of the priest is none other than the love that consumes him for humanity. In this the sacrament of the order and the sacrament of marriage are in intimate communion: **"That they may be one just as We are one, I in them and You in Me; that they may be made perfect in one and so that the world may know that You have sent Me and have loved them as You have loved Me"** (Jn 17:23).

CHAPTER VII

TOWARD A TRANSPARENT CONSCIOUSNESS

THE LORD IS IN THIS PLACE; AND I DID NOT KNOW IT (Gn 28:16)

The Fathers of the desert say that the greatest sin of all is forgetfulness of God. We are therefore faced with only one problem on the spiritual path: how to remain conscious of the divine Presence at all times. This is the only way to make progress in every moment.

Through Christ, God has entered into history, that is, into time and space; henceforth there is not a single place or moment that is not filled with His Presence. Jesus Christ brought about the end of a religion that was in the habit of sequestering God to prayer, worship or the temple. Now God is in everything: in every situation and in every event, within our family and professional relationships as much as in our moments of ecstacy, in our flesh and blood and even in the depths of our subconscious. Everything is through Him and in Him as Saint Paul constantly reminds us.

The great purpose of life, then, is not to accomplish this or that, but to encounter within all our successive activities, at the heart of every event, the God who waits for us there. Why is He there? What is He expecting of us? How is it that we live as though He does not exist? And isn't living in this way an enormous illusion? Have we ever truly discovered the incredible joy of being present to the moment? To ask oneself these questions every day is to examine our existence up close. Only in this way is our consciousness awakened and perhaps illumined on a whole other level still entirely unknown to us. How do we manage to break through toward this Life of plenitude? Humanity's universal Tradition responds: through the regular examination of conscience.

GOD PREPARES HIS COMING FROM ALL TIME

Long before the explicit incarnation of God in history, humanity had been preparing for it, stirred on by grace. All

212

people are called by God to live fully, whatever their tradition. But what answer do we give to this call? The continual adjustment of human beings toward God prepares from the beginning His distant Coming in history. Then the Divine-human communion will be complete. Already in Greco-Roman antiquity, Pythagoras and his disciples (sixth century B.C.) practiced the examination of conscience: "Do not allow," he would say, "gentle sleep to close your eyes before having examined each one of the actions of your day. What have I done wrong? What have I accomplished? What have I omitted that I should have done?" (*The Golden Verses*)

This practice widely used in antiquity is also found among a number of stoics such as Seneca: "Is there anything more beautiful than this custom of scrutinizing one's day. What sleep follows this examination of oneself, how peaceful, deep and free it is, when the spirit has been praised or warned, when it has made itself the secret censor of its own ways . . . I examine my whole day and measure my deeds and words; I hide nothing from myself, and let nothing go by." (*De Ira*)

Socrates (fifth century B.C.) recommends the famous

"Know thyself," to recognize the limits of one's being and to find humility before the gods. As for his disciple, Plato, he affirms that human beings will experience our true vocation if, through introspection, "we await a divine revelation."

The Taoist masters of China since Confucius (sixth century B.C.) had the sick undergo a meticulous examination of all their faults in order to find healing, even on the physical level. All sins from birth were to be put in writing and those who repented left healed. They knew that to purify onself is the preamble to all healing.

This is also the deep conviction of the religions of India. Both in the ancient tradition of the Hindu Brahmans and in Buddhism: to be healed one had to know that one was sick. "There is no tranquility for the one who does not persevere in the pursuit of the knowledge of self," says the Bhagavad-Gita. According to the sages, we are only capable of virtue if we have such knowledge. Monks and laypersons alike were led not only to know themselves and to judge the value of their actions, but also to clarify and strengthen their will through the discovery of the roots of evil in their hearts. The *watch of the heart* is the core of the examination

214

of conscience, especially among the Buddhists: "My spirit must be well supervised, well guarded: outside of the exercise of the watch of the spirit, what are all the others worth?" (Cautideva, *The Journey toward the Light*, sixth century).

Mystic muslems have made of the examination of conscience the master key in the spiritual battle: "O my brothers, dig into the most perfect of yourself and into the secrets in your chest, and purify them of all malice," writes Muhasibi. This return to oneself is done at the end of the day and affects all the movements of the soul. The soul must be examined day after day, hour by hour, in all its exterior and interior organs. The spiritual person aims at "the watch of the heart under the gaze of God who sees the hidden thoughts, knows the conscience and controls the actions of his servants" (Muhasibi). This requires the heart to undertake a constant turning and reaching out toward God.

THE HIGH PRECISION INSTRUMENT FOR THE JEW

With the muslems, we are already fully in the heritage of

the Israelite tradition. The Jewish soul has the examination of conscience bored into its innerds from its origins. Adam had hardly sinned when God interrogates his conscience through the famous question which, since then, resonates in the depths of every human being: "Adam, where are you?" Man, in the Old Testament, is in relationship only with God, he lives and walks only in His Presence (Gn 17:1). Life is a nuptial covenant with Him, a wedding where the present moment is the very location of the encounter. The examination of conscience, a high precision instrument for the Jew, has therefore no other interest than to bring into the light the wounds of love: "Prove me, O Lord, and try me; test my heart and my mind" (Psalm 26:2). And God, in love with humanity, effectively provokes the clear gaze upon oneself: "What right have you to recite My statutes, or take My covenant on your lips? If you see a thief, you are a friend of his; and you keep company with adulterers (Psalm 50:16-18). "You have not called upon Me, O Jacob; and you have been weary of Me, O Israel! . . . You have burdened Me with your sins, you have wearied Me with your iniquities . . . Put Me in remembrance, let us contend together; state your case, that you may be acquitted" (Isaiah 43:22-26).

We will never know what it is to live as long as we have not understood, through the divine revelation, that the Face of Love is inclined upon us moment by moment, and that only a single passion has the right to reign in our heart and within every one of our tasks: the passion to decipher the presence of this Face that knocks at the door of every instant. Along with many other texts in the Old Testament, the Song of Songs can make us dizzy from the revelation of a God so in love with us. He is the fiance forever on the look-out for his beloved creature; as every lover does, He seeks out the least gaze of humanity, a single moment of attention and the Heart of God is overwhelmed! Our consciousness cannot manage to grasp this wondrous Reality. This is precisely the urgency of examining it. The examination itself will be this "steep retreat" which the Song of Solomon speaks of, where consciousness increasingly awakens to love and says to the beloved: "Show me Your Face, let me hear Your Voice . . . Draw me after You, let us make haste!" (Song 2:14 and 1:4). This leads to the point where the gaze of our conscience is riveted on Him continually, because it cannot do otherwise as that is the very law of love: "O Lord, You have searched me and known me! You know my sitting down and my rising up; You understand my thought afar off. You comprehend my path and my lying down, and are acquainted with all my ways. For there is not a word on my tongue, but behold, O Lord, You know it altogether. You have hedged me behind and before, and laid Your hand upon me. Such knowledge is too wonderful for me; it is high, I cannot attain it." (Psalm 139)

THE TRANSPARENCE OF GOD IN THE CONSCIENCE OF HUMANITY

The examination of conscience aims at this complete reciprocity where human consciousness becomes more and more transparent to the consciousness of God, leading to a fusion without confusion, as with fire and iron. The infinity of God must become part of us, that is why we are *called*, and this is one of the first purposes of the examination of conscience as it leads us to discover how satisfied we are with the finite. But when we appease our thirst for the infinite through use of the finite, we are drinking in death and no happiness is possible for us. God has deposited in us and in all human traits—thought, joy, love—a capacity for infinite Divine consciousness, an aptitude to advance eternally in the infinity of God ever present within human consciousness. Holiness is nothing else than this reciprocal transparence between God and the individual, one containing the other. In the experience of this endless osmosis, man becomes god through divinization and God becomes man. Within this deepening without end, this always new experience, is found the substance of life, its true meaning and its only purpose. The transparence of the consciousness of God in that of human beings is visible on the face of those persons who are radiant as well as in their actions.

The more someone is transparent, the more he communicates this radiance through all his acts and gestures, especially with other people whose consciences then soak in the same Divine light. That is where our true responsibility to our brothers and sisters is secretly rooted. That is what is truly called *witness and mission:* there is no greater love than this mutual irradiation of the human family—through the light of God!

None of this is possible, however, if we let our soul

wander unbridled within the whim of circumstances and the anarchy of the unexpected. Only the clear and regular gaze can open our consciousness to a Beyond that inhabits us. A path opens up and, stage by stage, God Himself takes the opportunity to purify our conscience and to manifest the fact that we are never finished discovering Him. His mystery exceeds all reflection and our words cannot circumscribe Him.

Job best unveils this experience for us, as he undergoes his unbearable trial. Job is innocent and searches his conscience sincerely, "finding there no fault" (Job 31). It is during Job's search that God introduces the ultimate mutation: as metal is liquified in heat to become pure gold, so Job is tried to the core of his being, where nothing is left except his immovable decision to belong to God alone. Then his consciousness is illumined through the encounter of "a face" of God until then entirely unknown, and Job cries out: "I have heard of You by the hearing of the ear, but now my eye sees You" (Job 42:5). This is a new birth. One could go no further in the Old Testament.

JESUS CHRIST: THE ADVENT OF FREEDOM

We can say that Job is without doubt a remarkable prefiguration of Christ. Indeed, it is the cross of Christ which will definitively reveal the sin of humanity and allow the examination of conscience to go to the center of our alienation. From its very first pages, the Gospel places us face to face with this magnificent reality. John the Baptist announces in the same breath the salvation of the kingdom of God and the imperative necessity to face one's conscience (Luke 3:1-14). Jesus Himself will present the charter of John's message. The Sermon on the Mount (Matthew 5:7) is an immense examination of conscience where it finally reveals itself to be a new way of thinking. This is where history shifts, both universal history and our most personal one, through the advent of true human freedom.

Until then, for the Greeks and the Romans, freedom was the mastery of external circumstances, like a victorious mountain climber who overcomes the difficulties of a steep cliff. Jesus introduced a great rupture by showing that conscience is a participation in the creative act itself. God proposes that we join with Him to break through all limitations, in particular the supreme limit: death. The examination of conscience will now be the exercise leading to the content of this freedom where thought empties itself to belong to God alone. God leads us constantly from death to life at the heart of each infinitestimal detail of daily life, for that is where the Easter of Christ is played out.

There is nothing that is more developmental for our attitude, nothing more creative than to stand before one's life like the artist before a work to be brought into being. We can then stand before our life not as though it were a completed act (like a street that is simply there) but as a work in progress before a world entirely open. It is up to us to make our life a tomb or a dance of joy. That is the very role of art: to make visible the invisible. The world is not reducible to that which we can objectively see; it is possible to see in other ways and other things. There is nothing more constructive, more revolutionary than this freedom of expression that is proper to art. Every person is an artist and his masterpiece is himself. The examination of conscience serves as the instrument to generate our song. The examination of conscience places in our heart a tremendous surge of hope which Christ has introduced. A

Christ conscious heart is the true center of Christianity. With Jesus Christ, everything is possible (Luke 1:37) and the examination of conscience takes on a fundamentally prophetic function. Life is a perpetual birth: you must be born anew (John 3:3).

HOW TO DO AN EXAMINATION OF CONSCIENCE

This concrete undertaking since the Fathers of the desert to Saint Ignatius of Loyola, has been synthesized into five essential steps:

1) Give thanks for the blessings received during the day. The importance of this fundamental attitude cannot be overly stressed as it is the beginning of all true discernment. We have received the Spirit and His gifts and it is the spirit of joy which is suffocated if we are always displeased with ourselves, with others and with our life. Joy and gratitude should be the general atmosphere of the soul and must always be renewed, awakened, and deepened. Later we must give thanks for material and personal gifts that have come during the day. Nothing is to be taken for granted and

nothing is owed us: light, health, the air that we breathe, a child's laughter, a loved one's joy, a colleague's handshake, our work, our home, etc . . .

2) Ask God for the light to know the movements that have led us. In prayer, we must try to question our feelings, desires, repulsions, impulses, or blockages. What are the signs that the Spirit is making to us? How does He lead us? Toward what does He constantly attract us? This is a thread which goes through all our activities and is found beneath our psychic life and the movements of the soul. This is a discernment that needs to be continually refined.

3) Look at your thoughts, words, and deeds for the sake of becoming conscious, in the light of faith, of what has occured to you—and in you—during the day. The essential question is: how did the Father engender me today (Psalm 2:7) from thought to thought, action to action? What work did God accomplish in me? That is where, at the very heart of our spontaneous feelings, God leads us and deals with us in the most intimate way. These movements are studied in order to discern from what spirit they come. Little by little,

we learn to listen and to feel in every moment how God knocks at our door: love emerges minute by minute in very precise acts.

4) Ask forgiveness of God. The aim here is to learn that we are forgiven sinners. Nothing builds up praise more than this knowledge. Ask God to forgive us our many betrayals of love. Forgive others, love them as they are. Forgive events that are contrary to you, accept them, even when they are unacceptable, love (that is, bless) your enemies under whatever form they appear. Recurring forgiveness increasingly leads to a state of forgiveness, and the ego slowly disappears along with the tyranny of emotions. This leads to a stability in the soul that gives birth one day to impassiveness (*apatheia*), the sign of supreme freedom and of a joy that does not depend on external events.

5) In the light of the discernment that you have just done, how do you now see the future? Let the attitude live in you that you would like to have tomorrow, at work, under a certain circumstance or encounter. Then entrust yourself to God and surrender yourself to Him. It is He who will live through you.

The examination of conscience unifies us because it tests our deepest desire. This is the whole point. It has meaning only for the one who seeks to make inner progress. That is why the great saints held to the examination more than to prayer. It is possible for them to reduce the time given to prayer if necessary, but never to drop the examination!

The examination is done in the evening, but it is very fruitful to perform it briefly in the midst of the day, where in the blink of an eye we can look at the point on which the spiritual effort will have its maximum intensity, whether it is a weakness to overcome or a fundamental attitude that we seek to adopt.

Thanks to this work, the examination becomes an almost continuous state of watchfulness: "a watch of the heart such that not the least unruly movement occurs without our noticing it and immediately correcting it" (P. Lallemant).

In this recollection toward the interior, watchfulness and perpetual prayer ultimately become one.

About the Author

ALPHONSE and **RACHEL GOETTMANN** are the directors of Béthanie, a Center of Hesychast Meditation, Bible and Tradition, located in eastern France near the city of Metz. Father Goettmann is a priest in the Orthodox Church of France. They are the publishers of the quarterly journal *Le Chemin* and have co-authored a number of books, including *Prayer of Jesus—Prayer of the Heart, The Beyond Within: Initiation into Christian Meditation,* and *Dialogue on the Path of Initiation: An Introduction to the Life and Thought of Karlfried Graf Dürckheim.* The Goettmanns lead numerous retreats throughout the year at their center.

Made in the USA
San Bernardino, CA
05 June 2019